THE SLOWCOOKER LIBRARY
Convenience Foods for Singles

THE SLOWCOOKER LIBRARY
Convenience Foods for Singles

Catherine Atkinson

foulsham

LONDON • NEW YORK • TORONTO • SYDNEY

foulsham

The Oriel, Thames Valley Court, 183–187 Bath Road, Slough,
Berkshire SL1 4AA, England

Foulsham books can be found in all good bookshops and direct from
www.foulsham.com

ISBN: 978-0-572-03533-4

Copyright © 2010 W. Foulsham & Co. Ltd

Cover photograph © Fresh Food Images

A CIP record for this book is available from the British Library

Printed in Great Britain by Printwise (Haverhill) Ltd, Haverhill

contents

Introduction 7

Choosing a slow cooker 9

Using & caring for your slow cooker 10

Cooking times 12

Adapting your own recipes 14

Slow cooker safety 15

Slow cooking hints & tips 17

Notes on the recipes 19

Soups 20

Light meals 42

Seafood 60

Beef, lamb & pork 88

Chicken, turkey & duck 154

Vegetarian 192

Desserts & cakes 226

Index 250

introduction

At the end of a busy day you are very likely to be tired, hungry and looking forward to sitting down and enjoying a meal. Rather than dashing out for a takeaway or settling for a chilled ready-made meal from a packet, wouldn't it be great to serve a delicious and nutritious home-cooked meal from your slow cooker?

Whether you live alone or simply find you will be having a solitary night in, cooking can be a chore. Slow cooking is the perfect way to create flavour-packed meals with the minimum effort and fuss. Ideal for soups, casseroles, vegetables and desserts, this method of cooking means you can prepare meals in advance and leave them unattended to cook for as many hours as they need. The drawback with so many slow cooker cookbooks is that most recipes require time-consuming preparation and include pre-frying ingredients such as onions and meat – not something you often feel like doing first thing in the morning, or before going out for the day or off to work.

While the meals in this book make the most of fresh foods, they also take advantage of time-saving ready-prepared ingredients such as garlic and ginger purées (pastes), and frozen vegetables including diced onions, sliced mushrooms and (bell) peppers. The fresh equivalent is also given, so you can use whichever you prefer. Cans and jars of prepared ingredients also feature in the recipes, including cooked beans and pulses, fried onions and ready-made white sauce.

The basic principle behind the slow cooker is that it cooks food slowly at a constant temperature. This has many advantages, one of the greatest being that it develops and enhances the flavour of food, while retaining its texture. It makes even the toughest meat meltingly tender – in fact, the less expensive cuts are better suited to slow cooking. Slow cookers are also environmentally friendly; their low wattage consumes about the same amount of electricity as a light bulb. They can save up to five times the energy of stove-top and conventional oven cooking, making them ideal for those on a budget. The essentials of slow cooking are incredibly simple, but do have a look at the following pages before you start to use the recipes.

All the recipes in this book have been created to use a range of ingredients that are easy to buy on a small scale, so you don't have to worry about spending a fortune on unwanted food. They are designed for one, but many make two servings – one to serve straight away and one that can be jazzed up for the following day, or frozen for a later date – saving both time and money. There are mouth-watering meals to suit every occasion from light lunches and midweek meals to delectable desserts and indulgent cakes. Solo eating has never been simpler or more enjoyable!

choosing a slow cooker

Slow cookers come in a wide selection of sizes, shapes, colours and prices and these factors need to be considered before you decide which one is right for you. Appearance is the first thing you'll notice; you'll find contemporary stainless steel, rich-coloured and pristine-looking white models as well as the rustic-looking cream and brown versions. Originally only round slow cookers were available; these are excellent for soup and casserole making and for cooking puddings in basins and cakes in round tins. The more modern oval version is a better buy if you entertain often as it's perfect for pot-roasting larger joints of meat and is also good for cooking loaf-shaped cakes and pâtés.

When slow cookers were first manufactured, the ceramic cooking pots were permanently fixed into the outer casing. You may still have such a slow cooker, but more recent models have a removable cooking pot that fits into an outer metal casing. The heating elements are safely situated between the inner and outer casings. A removable cooking pot can be used as a serving dish and allows food to be browned in the oven or under the grill (broiler) without causing damage to the outer casing. It also simplifies washing up. The heat-resistant lid may be ceramic or toughened glass. The latter allows you to monitor the food without lifting the lid and losing precious heat.

The size of slow cookers ranges from a tiny 600 ml/1 pint/$2\frac{1}{2}$ cup cooking pot to a massive 6.5 litre/$11\frac{1}{2}$ pint/$26\frac{1}{4}$ cup one. I have found the ideal size to be 1.5 litres/$2\frac{1}{2}$ pint/6 cups – a large enough capacity for two portions, but small enough to ensure that food such as portions of fish or meat will fit snugly inside and be sufficiently covered by the cooking liquid. This size is a great asset for singles and couples and takes up very little space in the kitchen.

using & caring for your slow cooker

Because slow cooker models vary, make sure you read the manufacturer's guide book before using yours for the first time. Some slow cookers need to be preheated before you start cooking, but most advise against heating the slow cooker when empty. You should also check to see whether your ceramic cooking pot is dishwasher-proof and whether it can be used under the grill (broiler) and in the oven, in the microwave or in the freezer.

Always remove any labels and tags from a new slow cooker, then wash the ceramic cooking pot in hot soapy water, rinse well and dry. You may notice a slight odour as the slow cooker heats up; this is caused by the burning off of manufacturing residues and will lessen and eventually disappear after a few uses. After several months, the glaze on the cooking pot may become slightly crazed; this is perfectly normal and will not affect the slow cooker's efficiency.

You will notice that many of the recipes here advise using hot (not boiling) water and stock when adding it straight to the cooking pot; never pour boiling liquid into the cold cooking pot (you can do so when it is already warm or hot) or plunge it into cold water immediately after use as this could crack it. Remember that it is an electrical appliance, so the outer casing should only be wiped clean with a damp soapy cloth (never use scouring pads or abrasive cleaners) and never be immersed in or filled with water.

When following a recipe, bear in mind that every slow cooker model is slightly different and, even when using the same settings, some will cook much faster than others. For this reason a range of cooking times is usually given; you may need to use the shorter or the longer time, or somewhere between the two. After trying a few recipes, you will know whether your slow cooker is faster or slower and you will be able to adjust the recipe cooking times accordingly.

cooking times

The cooking temperatures and settings vary on different models, but most have four settings: Low, High, Auto and Off. Some models have an additional Medium setting. At the lowest temperature the food should barely simmer: at the highest it will boil very gently.

Use the Low setting when you want to cook food for an extended time without overcooking or burning.

When set to Auto, the cooking temperature will build up to High (the time this takes depends on the quantity of food being cooked and its initial temperature), then remain at this temperature for an hour or so before automatically switching to Low. This setting is desirable if you are using frozen vegetables in your cooking without defrosting them first. Foods such as poultry joints (chicken quarters and whole thighs, for example, but not breasts or chopped chicken) and cakes should be always be cooked on High or Auto. Food should be monitored when using the High setting as some liquid will evaporate.

Some flexibility can be introduced to the total cooking time by adjusting the temperature settings; for dishes such as soups, braises and casseroles, the cooking can be shortened or extended to suit your needs by changing the temperature setting. As a rough guide, the cooking time on Low is about double that of High.

Low	Auto or Medium	High
2–4	$1\frac{1}{2}$–$2\frac{1}{2}$	1–2
6–8	4–6	3–4
8–10	6–8	5–6

If at the end of the cooking time the food is not quite ready, replace the lid and switch the setting to High to speed up the cooking process. Once ready, many dishes, especially casseroles and soups, can be kept hot for an hour or more without any risk of spoiling by switching the temperature to Low.

If you are planning to go out for the day and your chosen recipe does not take as many hours to cook as you will be away, you can use a time-delay plug so that the start of cooking is delayed by several hours. This is particularly useful if you are including a large quantity of frozen vegetables, which will then have a chance to thaw during this time and come up to room temperature before cooking starts. It's important that all the ingredients – including stock – are cold (preferably chilled) when added to the ceramic cooking pot. However, never use a time-delay plug when cooking chicken or when the kitchen will be warm, for instance on a sunny day, or if the central heating will be on before cooking commences.

Modern slow cookers tend to cook at a slightly higher temperature than those that are 10 or more years old so, if you have a newer model, check whether the food is ready at the minimum suggested cooking time when following the first few recipes.

adapting your own recipes

Many conventional recipes can be adapted for cooking in a slow cooker. The easiest way to adapt a recipe is find a similar one in this book and use it as a guide to modify the original recipe.

Remember that there is less evaporation in the slow cooker than in conventional cooking so reduce the liquid content by about a third. Check towards the end of cooking time and add more boiling liquid if the dish is looking dry.

Since vegetables tend to cook more slowly than meat, make sure they are at the bottom of the slow cooker and chopped more finely.

slow cooker safety

The slow cooker is an extremely safe appliance, but common-sense precautions should always be followed. Although it cooks at a low temperature, the outer casing, lid and the food inside the slow cooker may get extremely hot, so you should always use oven gloves when removing the ceramic cooking pot. Stand the slow cooker on a heat-resistant surface when in use, not near the edge where it might accidentally get knocked off, and make sure that the mains lead is tucked safely behind it. Take extra care that it's out of reach if you have young children or inquisitive pets living or staying with you.

Slow cookers cook food at a relatively low heat – around 90°C/195°F on the Low setting to about 150°C/300°F on the High setting. Any bacteria present in food is destroyed at 74°C/165°F so, as long as it's cooked for the correct time, the temperature of the slow cooker will ensure that the food is safe to eat. You should take care, however, not to reduce the cooking temperature:

- Do not lift the lid during the cooking time unless the recipe specifies this.
- Ideally ingredients should be at room temperature when you start to cook. If you are using a large quantity of frozen vegetables, it's a good idea to set the slow cooker on High or Auto for the first hour of cooking. Never add frozen or part-frozen meat or poultry to the slow cooker.
- You may need to increase the cooking time slightly when the kitchen temperature is extremely cold.
- Avoid placing the slow cooker in a cold room, in a draughty place or near an open window.

Always check that meat is thoroughly cooked, particularly poultry and pork. A meat thermometer is a good investment if you cook portions or joints of meat as it will ensure they are sufficiently cooked without drying out and losing moistness. The meat is ready when the pointer on the dial reaches the appropriate wording; there are indications for types of meat including chicken, beef, lamb and pork, as well as readings within some of those categories for rare, medium and well-cooked meat.

slow cooking hints & tips

- **Keep the lid on:** During cooking, steam condenses on the lid of the slow cooker, then trickles back into the pot, helping to retain heat and reduce strong cooking smells. Make sure that the lid is placed centrally on the cooking pot. Unless a recipe tells you to stir a dish part-way through cooking, it should be left undisturbed and you should avoid lifting the lid. If you do need to lift the lid during cooking other than when specified in a recipe (to add a forgotten ingredient, for instance), add an extra 10–15 minutes to the cooking time to make up for the heat loss.
- **Don't overfill the pot:** Allow a 5 cm/2 in distance between the food and top of the ceramic cooking pot, particularly with food that requires simmering such as soups and casseroles. While all of the recipes here follow this (if cooked in a two-portion sized slow cooker), bear this in mind if you decide to double the ingredients in a recipe for entertaining or for freezing in individual portions.
- **Use alcohol sparingly:** Alcohol evaporates more slowly in the slow cooker, so use only a small amount or the flavour may be overpoweringly alcoholic.
- **Cook root vegetables at the bottom:** Onions and root vegetables such as carrots take longer to cook than meat as the liquid simmers rather than boils. These should be cut into smallish, even-sized chunks before adding to the cooking pot. If possible, place them at the bottom of the cooking pot, which is the hottest part, and make sure they are completely immersed in liquid.
- **Add onions while you prepare ingredients:** In many of the recipes in this book, the onions are added with hot stock and the slow cooker switched on while you are measuring and preparing

the rest of the ingredients. This allows the onions to warm through and starts the cooking process.

- **Add other vegetables at the end:** Vegetables with a high water content such as pumpkins and courgettes (zucchini) will cook quickly, so add them towards the end of cooking time, or place them towards the top of the cooking pot rather than nearer the base, where the temperature is higher.

- **Defrost frozen vegetables:** It is preferable for frozen vegetables to be thawed before adding, but it isn't essential. If time allows, defrost them in the fridge for several hours or overnight or spread them out on kitchen paper (paper towels) at room temperature. If adding frozen vegetables, the dish will take a little longer to cook than if thawed ones are used.

- **Use easy-cook rice:** Ordinary long-grain rice doesn't cook well in the slow cooker, but easy-cook (converted) rice, also known as 'parboiled', will cook to perfection. It has been steamed under pressure, ensuring the grains remain separate and making it difficult to overcook. Easy-cook brown and easy-cook basmati rice are also readily available.

- **Choose durum wheat pasta:** When cooking pasta in the slow cooker, choose dried pasta made from 100 per cent durum wheat as it will retain its shape and texture better than egg pasta. Fresh pasta does not cook successfully.

- **Check the pot size:** When cooking pâtés, cakes or desserts in tins or dishes in the slow cooker, always make sure first that they will fit as most cooking pots taper slightly towards the base. Place the tin or dish on an upturned saucer or a metal pastry (paste) cutter, so that the simmering water can circulate underneath and all around.

- **Choose when to add your herbs:** Fresh herbs added at the beginning of long cooking will lose their colour, texture and pungency. Use dried herbs at the start of cooking and add fresh ones towards the end.

notes on the recipes

- Do not mix metric, imperial and American measures. Follow one set only.
- All spoon measurements are level: 1 tsp = 5 ml; 1 tbsp = 15 ml.
- American terms are given in brackets.
- The ingredients are listed in the order in which they are used in the recipe.
  Eggs are medium unless otherwise stated. If you use a different size, adjust the amount of liquid added to obtain the right consistency.
- Always wash, peel, core and seed, if necessary, fresh fruit and vegetables before use. Ensure that all produce is as fresh as possible and in good condition.
- The use of strongly flavoured ingredients such as fresh garlic, chilli and ginger depends on personal taste and quantities can be adjusted accordingly.
- All cooking times are approximate and are intended as a guide only. Get to know your slow cooker; you will soon know if it cooks a little faster or slower than the times given here.
- Can and packet sizes are approximate and will depend on the particular brand.
- Vegetarian recipes are marked with a symbol. Those who eat fish but not meat will find plenty of additional recipes containing seafood to enjoy. Some vegetarian recipes contain dairy products; substitute with a vegetarian alternative if you prefer. Recipes may also use processed foods, and vegetarians should check the specific product labels to be certain of their suitability, especially items such as stocks and sauces.

V
Suitable for
vegetarians

soups

No canned, packet or carton variety can rival a bowl of delicious home-made soup made with fresh ingredients and usually at a fraction of the price. Plus the slow cooker is the ideal way to cook them – long and slow – for maximum flavour.

In this chapter, you'll find classic soups from all round the world, including French Onion (see pages 38–9), Hungarian Sausage (see pages 26–7) and Chicken Masala (see pages 36–7). All can be served as light lunch or supper dishes, or complemented with bread when you want something a bit more substantial.

Soup tips

- The secret of a successful soup often lies in a well-flavoured stock, so if you haven't the time or inclination to make your own, choose a good-quality commercial one.

- You can make your own stock in the slow cooker with leftover bones and vegetables, boiling water and a bouquet garni, left on Low all day.

- Take care not to over-season soups – especially if you have used a ready-made stock, as some already have a high salt content.

- As you lose so little liquid during cooking, add two-thirds of the liquid when adapting conventional recipes.

- You can thicken with cream, milk or egg yolks for the last 30 minutes of cooking time.

- If necessary, thin down with boiling water or stock.

- Vary the recipes to suit what is in season.

mixed vegetable soup

Chef's note

Almost any vegetable can be made into soup and this simple recipe can be used as a guide. For a change, try adding broccoli, courgettes (zucchini), parsnips, turnips, swede (rutabaga) or sweet potatoes, cutting them into even-sized pieces to ensure they are all tender at the same time.

4-6 hrs
LOW

Wholemeal toast or crusty bread rolls

1 small **onion**, very finely chopped, or 30 ml/2 tbsp **frozen diced onion**

450 ml/¾ pint/2 cups very hot (not boiling) **vegetable stock**

350 g/12 oz **fresh mixed vegetables** such as carrots, celery and potatoes or **frozen chopped mixed vegetables**

1 **bay leaf**

5 ml/1 tsp **dried mixed herbs**

Salt and freshly ground black pepper

30 ml/2 tbsp **milk** or **single (light) cream** (optional)

1   Put the onion in the ceramic cooking pot. Pour the stock over, cover with the lid and switch on the slow cooker to Low. Leave to warm for 3–4 minutes while measuring and preparing the remaining ingredients.

2   If using fresh vegetables, cut into 5 mm/¼ in slices or dice. Add the fresh or frozen vegetables to the ceramic cooking pot with the bay leaf and sprinkle the dried herbs over.

3   Re-cover with the lid and cook for 4–6 hours or until all the vegetables are tender. Remove the bay leaf and season to taste with salt and pepper. Transfer half the soup to a bowl or a freezer container and allow to cool.

4   If using milk or cream, stir this into the remaining soup and cook for a further 15 minutes to bring the soup back to boiling point. (Do not heat for longer than this, as long cooking may cause the soup to separate). Taste and re-season, if necessary, then serve in a warm bowl with wholemeal toast or crusty rolls.

Second serving

• Either cover the cooled soup and chill in the fridge for the following day, or freeze for up to a month. If frozen, allow the soup to defrost in the fridge overnight. To serve, transfer to a saucepan and heat until piping hot.

Cook's tips

• If you are using vegetables with a high water content such as courgettes or squash, reduce the quantity of stock a little. If you are using a high proportion of vegetables such as potatoes that soak up cooking juices, or adding dried vegetables, add a little more liquid to compensate.

chilli bean chowder

2

4-6 hrs LOW

Wholemeal toast or crusty bread rolls

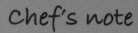

Chef's note

Protein-packed beans form the basis of this substantial soup. Made mainly from storecupboard ingredients, it's up to you whether you make it hot and spicy as here, or go for a milder flavour by reducing the amount of chilli.

V

Suitable for Vegetarians

1 **red onion**, finely chopped, or 30 ml/2 tbsp **frozen diced onion**

1 **garlic clove**, crushed, or 5 ml/1 tsp **garlic purée** (paste)

250 ml/8 fl oz/1 cup boiling **vegetable stock**

A large pinch of crushed dried **chilli flakes** or 2.5 ml/½ tsp **chilli powder**

1.5 ml/¼ tsp **ground coriander**

1.5 ml/¼ tsp **ground cumin**

150 ml/¼ pint/⅔ cup **tomato juice**

½ × 400 g/14 oz/large can of **mixed beans** or **red kidney beans**, drained and rinsed

Salt and freshly ground black pepper

1   Put the onion and garlic in the ceramic cooking pot. Pour the stock over, cover with the lid and switch on the slow cooker to Low. Leave for a few minutes while measuring and preparing the remaining ingredients.

2   Add the chilli, coriander, cumin, tomato juice and beans. Stir, then re-cover with the lid and cook for 5–7 hours until the onion is very tender.

3   Ladle about two-thirds of the soup into a blender or liquidiser and purée until completely smooth. Return to the cooking pot and stir well, then transfer half the soup to a bowl or freezer container and allow to cool.

4   Reheat the remaining soup on High for 15 minutes or until piping hot or quickly reheat in a saucepan on the hob. Season to taste with salt and pepper and serve in a warm bowl with hot toast or crusty bread rolls.

Second serving

• Either cover the cooled soup and chill in the fridge for the following day, or freeze for up to a month. If frozen, allow the soup to defrost in the fridge overnight. To serve, transfer to a saucepan and heat until piping hot.

Cook's tips

• To make a more substantial meal, serve the soup topped with a spoonful of thick natural yoghurt and a sprinkling of grated Manchego or Cheddar cheese. Accompany with some tortilla chips.

hungarian sausage soup

2

4-6 hrs LOW

Pumpkin seed or other seeded bread

This is a substantial main-meal soup, packed with chunky vegetables. As it slowly cooks, the potatoes soak up the flavour of the smoked sausage and paprika and thicken the soup, making the perfect welcome home on a cold day.

1 small **onion**, chopped, or 30 ml/2 tbsp **frozen diced onion**

250 ml/8 fl oz/1 cup very hot (not boiling) **beef stock**

1 small red or yellow (bell) **pepper** or 150 g/5 oz **frozen mixed sliced peppers**

175 g/6 oz **potato**, diced

5 ml/1 tsp **ground paprika**

1.5 ml/¼ tsp **caraway seeds** (optional)

½ × 225 g/8 oz packet of **smoked pork sausage**, sliced

200 g/7 oz/small can of **chopped tomatoes**

Salt and freshly ground black pepper

1. Put the onion in the ceramic cooking pot. Pour the stock over, cover with the lid and switch on the slow cooker to Low. Leave to warm for a few minutes while measuring and preparing the rest of the ingredients.

2. If using a fresh pepper, quarter it and remove the white core and seeds. Cut each quarter into thin slices. Add the pepper, potato, paprika, caraway seeds, if using, sausage slices and tomatoes to the cooking pot. Season with salt and pepper.

3. Re-cover with the lid and cook for 4–6 hours or until the peppers and potatoes are very tender. Taste and re-season, if necessary, then transfer half the soup to a bowl or freezer container and allow to cool.

4. Serve the remaining soup in a warm bowl accompanied by buttered slices of pumpkin seed or seeded bread.

Second serving

- Either cover the cooled soup and chill in the fridge for the following day, or freeze for up to a month. If frozen, allow the soup to defrost in the fridge overnight. To serve, transfer to a saucepan and heat until piping hot.

Cook's tip

- There are several types of smoked pork sausage available including garlic-flavoured and a reduced-fat version. All would be suitable for this recipe.

classic vichyssoise

2

5-7 hrs
LOW

Extra double cream
or crème fraîche
(optional) and melba
toast or breadsticks

15 g/½ oz/1 tbsp **butter**

1 **leek**, trimmed and sliced

1 **potato**, about 175 g/6 oz, peeled and cut into chunks

1 **bay leaf**

5 ml/1 tsp **lemon juice**

450 ml/¾ pint/2 cups very hot (not boiling) **vegetable stock**

75 ml/5 tbsp **double (heavy) cream**

Salt and white pepper

1   Put the butter in the ceramic cooking pot and switch on the slow cooker to Low. Leave for a few minutes until melted while measuring and preparing the rest of the ingredients.

2   Add the leeks to the pot and stir to coat in the butter. Scatter the potato chunks on top, add the bay leaf and lemon juice, then pour the stock over the vegetables. Cover with the lid and cook for 5–7 hours or until the vegetables are very tender.

3   Discard the bay leaf. Allow the soup to cool slightly, then purée with a hand blender in the cooking pot or in a blender or food processor until smooth. Pour the soup into a bowl and leave to cool, then cover and chill in the fridge for at least 4 hours.

4   Stir in the cream and season to taste with salt and pepper. Ladle half the soup into a chilled bowl, add a swirl of cream or crème fraiche, if liked, and serve with melba toast or breadsticks.

Second serving
• Either cover the remaining cooled soup and chill in the fridge for the following day, or freeze for up to a month. If frozen, allow the soup to defrost in the fridge overnight. After defrosting, the soup may have a slightly separated appearance or appear to have 'split'; this can be remedied by whisking until smooth.

Cook's tips
• Vichyssoise may also be served hot as leek and potato soup. Add milk to the soup instead of cream.
• Check the consistency of the soup before serving. A little extra stock, milk or cream may be added to thin it, if desired.

wild mushroom soup

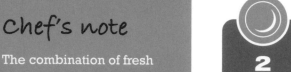

2

4-5 hrs
LOW

Crème fraîche
or soured (dairy
sour) cream
Crusty bread

15 g/½ oz/¼ cup dried **wild mushrooms**, such as porcini, morels or ceps

450 ml/¾ pint/2 cups hot (not boiling) **vegetable stock**

1 small **onion**, finely chopped, or 25 g/1 oz **frozen diced onion**

1 **garlic clove**, crushed, or 5 ml/1 tsp **garlic purée** (paste)

225 g/8 oz fresh or **frozen sliced button mushrooms**

15 ml/1 tbsp **Madeira** or dry sherry

A pinch of **dried mixed herbs**

A pinch of freshly grated **nutmeg** (optional)

Salt and freshly ground black pepper

1   Put the dried mushrooms in a sieve (strainer) and rinse under cold running water to remove any grit. Put them in the ceramic cooking pot with the stock. Cover with the lid and switch on the slow cooker to Low. Leave for a few minutes while measuring and preparing the rest of the ingredients.

2   Add the onion, garlic, sliced mushrooms, Madeira or sherry, the herbs and nutmeg, if using. Season generously with salt and pepper, then re-cover with the lid and cook for 4–5 hours or until the mushrooms are very tender.

3   Purée the soup in a food processor or blender until smooth. Transfer half the soup to a bowl or freezer container and cool.

4   Return the remaining soup to the cooking pot and heat on High for about 15 minutes until piping hot (or quickly reheat in a saucepan on the hob). Taste and re-season, if necessary, then serve in a warm bowl, topped with crème fraîche or soured cream and accompanied by crusty bread or hot buttered toast.

Second serving

- Either cover the cooled soup and chill in the fridge for the following day, or freeze for up to a month. If frozen, allow the soup to defrost in the fridge overnight. To serve, transfer to a saucepan and heat on the hob until piping hot.

butter bean and pesto soup

2

3-5 hrs
LOW

Crusty bread or
hot buttered
toast

Chef's note

This substantial and nutritious soup is perfect for lunch or supper, served with warm bread or toast. Green pesto – a sauce based on basil and Parmesan cheese – is added just before serving and turns this simple soup into something special.

V

Suitable for
Vegetarians

1 small **onion**, chopped, or 30 ml/2 tbsp **frozen diced onion**

175 g/6 oz **frozen mixed vegetables**

400 g/14 oz/large can of **butter (lima) beans**, drained and rinsed

450 ml/¾ pint/2 cups very hot (not boiling) **vegetable stock**

Salt and freshly ground black pepper

30 ml/2 tbsp **green pesto sauce**

1   Put the onion, mixed vegetables and beans in the ceramic cooking pot. Pour the stock over and season with salt and pepper.

2   Switch on the slow cooker to Low. Cover with the lid and cook for 3–5 hours or until the vegetables are really tender.

3   Purée the soup in a food processor or with a hand-held blender until smooth and creamy, then stir in the pesto. Transfer half the soup to a bowl or freezer container and allow to cool.

4   Return the remaining soup to the pot and heat on High for about 15 minutes until piping hot or quickly reheat in a saucepan on the hob. Taste and re-season, if necessary, then serve in a warm bowl accompanied by crusty bread or hot buttered toast.

Second serving

• Either cover the cooled soup and chill in the fridge for the following day, or freeze for up to a month. If frozen, allow the soup to defrost in the fridge overnight. To serve, transfer to a saucepan and heat through.

Cook's tip

• Choose your favourite type of frozen mixed vegetables for this soup: carrots, peas, green beans and sweetcorn are a typical combination; others containing broccoli and red (bell) pepper would also work well.

rich lentil and tomato soup

2

4-6 hrs **LOW**

Bread rolls or hot buttered toast

Lentils are high in protein and contain good amounts of iron, zinc and B-vitamins. Combined with canned tomatoes, rich in antioxidants, this wholesome soup with a vibrant colour makes a delicious starter or light meal.

V

Suitable for vegetarians

1 small **onion**, finely chopped, or 30 ml/2 tbsp **frozen diced onion**

350 ml/12 fl oz/1⅓ cups very hot (not boiling) **vegetable stock**

75 g/3 oz/½ cup split **red lentils**

200 g/7 oz/small can of **chopped tomatoes**

15 ml/1 tbsp **sun-dried tomato purée** (paste)

1 **celery stick**, finely chopped

1 **carrot**, finely diced, or 75 g/ 3 oz **frozen diced carrots**

1 **bay leaf**

A pinch of **dried mixed herbs**

Salt and freshly ground black pepper

1   Put the onion into the ceramic cooking pot. Pour the stock over, cover with the lid and switch on the slow cooker to Low. Leave to warm for 3–4 minutes while measuring and preparing the rest of the ingredients.

2   Rinse the lentils in a sieve under cold running water, then add to the pot with the tomatoes, tomato purée, celery, carrot, bay leaf and herbs. Stir well, then re-cover with the lid and cook for 4–6 hours.

3   Discard the bay leaf. Leave the soup chunky or, if preferred, purée with a hand-held blender or in a food processor until completely smooth. Transfer half the soup to a bowl or freezer container and allow to cool.

4   Return the remaining soup to the pot and heat on High for about 15 minutes until piping hot or quickly reheat in a saucepan on the hob. Season to taste with salt and pepper and serve in a warm bowl with bread rolls or hot buttered toast.

Second serving

• Either cover the cooled soup and chill for the following day, or freeze for up to a month. If frozen, allow the soup to defrost in the fridge overnight. To serve, transfer to a saucepan and heat until piping hot.

Cook's tips

• If you don't want to use celery, simply leave it out or use celery salt as a seasoning instead of ordinary salt.
• You can spice up the second serving, if you like, by stirring in 5 ml/ 1 tsp of your favourite curry paste. After reheating, top the soup with a tablespoonful of thick yoghurt and serve with warmed naan bread or ready-made popadoms.
• This is quite a thick soup, especially if puréed. Add a little more stock or milk if you prefer a thinner consistency.

chicken masala soup

2

3-5 hrs
LOW

Chapattis or
naan bread

Chef's note

Indian spices add warmth and colour to this delicious dish, which is a cross between a soup and a stew. A steaming bowlful topped with a dollop of thick natural yoghurt and a sprinkling of chopped fresh coriander is sure to please.

1 small **onion**, chopped, or 30 ml/2 tbsp **frozen diced onion**

1 **garlic clove**, crushed, or 5 ml/1 tsp **garlic purée** (paste)

2.5 ml/½ tsp **ground coriander**

2.5 ml/½ tsp **ground cumin**

1.5 ml/¼ tsp **ground turmeric**

1.5 ml/¼ tsp **ground ginger**

250 ml/8 fl oz/1 cup very hot (not boiling) **chicken stock**

225 g/8 oz **chicken breast** or **mini chicken fillets**

200 g/7 oz/small can of **chopped tomatoes**

100 g/4 oz fresh or frozen **green beans**, halved

½ × 400 g/14 oz/large can of **chick peas** (garbanzos), drained and rinsed

15 ml/1 tbsp fresh or frozen **chopped coriander** (cilantro)

Salt and freshly ground black pepper

1   Put the onion, garlic, ground coriander, cumin, turmeric and ginger in the ceramic cooking pot and turn the slow cooker on to Low.

2   Pour the stock over, cover with the lid and leave for a few minutes while measuring and preparing the rest of the ingredients.

3   Cut the chicken into 2 cm/¾ in wide strips. Add to the pot with the tomatoes, beans and chick peas. Re-cover with the lid and cook for 3–5 hours or until the chicken is tender and the vegetables are cooked. Stir in the chopped coriander and season to taste with salt and pepper.

4   Spoon half of the soup into a bowl or freezer container and leave to cool. Ladle the rest into a warm bowl and serve straight away with chapattis or naan bread.

Second serving

- Either cover the cooled soup and chill in the fridge for the following day, or freeze for up to a month. If frozen, allow to defrost in the fridge overnight. To serve, heat gently in a saucepan and allow to bubble for a few minutes until piping hot.

Cook's tips

- To save time, use 7.5 ml/1½ tsp of your favourite curry powder or paste instead of the individual dry spices.
- Extra vegetables may be added, if liked, such as diced courgette (zucchini) or canned or frozen sweetcorn.
- Use leftover chick peas for Harissa-spiced Chick Peas (see page 54).

french onion soup

2

1½-3 hrs
LOW

Small French
stick and grated
cheese

Chef's note

When making French onion soup on a hob, the onions are slowly cooked until lightly caramelised, involving time and frequent stirring. This is an amazingly simple yet authentic-tasting version made using a can of ready-fried onions.

V

Suitable for
Vegetarians

400 g/14 oz/large can of **fried onions in olive oil**

415 g/14½ oz/large can of **beef consommé**

120 ml/4 fl oz/½ cup **dry white wine**

1 small **garlic clove**, crushed, or 2.5 ml/½ tsp **garlic purée** (paste)

1 **bay leaf**

Salt and freshly ground black pepper

1 Put all the ingredients in the ceramic cooking pot, give them a stir, then switch on the slow cooker to Low. Cover with the lid and cook for 1½–3 hours.

2 Just before serving, lightly toast the French bread slices on both sides under a moderate grill (broiler). Sprinkle one side thickly with the cheese, then grill until golden brown and bubbling.

3 Remove the bay leaf from the soup, taste and re-season, if necessary. Transfer half the soup to a bowl or freezer container and allow to cool. Serve the remaining soup in a warm bowl with a piece of the cheese on toast floating on the top and the rest served separately.

Second serving

- Either cover the cooled soup and chill in the fridge for the following day, or freeze for up to a month. If frozen, allow the soup to defrost in the fridge overnight. To serve, transfer to a saucepan and heat until piping hot. Instead of the toasted cheese topping, serve the soup with bought garlic croûtons.

Cook's tips

- This dish is perfect for entertaining as it can be prepared about an hour before your guest arrives, then left to bubble gently. You can also toast the French bread beforehand and top with the cheese. Grill the cheese-topped slices when you are ready to eat.
- You can buy jars and tubes of garlic purée in the supermarket. It's especially good for those recipes when you want only a tiny amount of garlic and once opened will keep in the fridge for 2–3 months.

split pea and squash soup

Chef's note

Long, slow cooking brings out all the rich flavour of butternut squash and sweet potato to create this beautiful golden-coloured soup. Although this recipe requires forward planning as the split peas need pre-soaking, using a packet of ready diced vegetables makes preparation easy.

V

Suitable for vegetarians

2

3-7 hrs
LOW

Crusty
wholemeal
bread

75 g/3 oz/½ cup **yellow split peas**

1 **onion**, finely chopped, or 40 g/1½ oz **frozen diced onion**

450 ml/¾ pint/2 cups very hot (not boiling) **vegetable stock**

300 g/11 oz packet of **diced butternut squash and sweet potatoes**

1.5 ml/¼ tsp **ground turmeric**

1 **bay leaf**

Salt and freshly ground black pepper

1   Put the split peas in a bowl, cover with plenty of cold water and leave to soak for at least 3 hours, or overnight if preferred.

2   Put the onion in the ceramic cooking pot and pour the stock over. Switch on the slow cooker to Auto or Low. Drain the split peas and add to the pot with the butternut squash and sweet potatoes, the turmeric and bay leaf. Cover with the lid and cook for 3–5 hours on Auto or 5–7 hours on Low.

3   Discard the bay leaf, then purée the soup with a hand-held blender in the cooking pot or in a food processor until smooth. Transfer half the soup to a bowl or freezer container and allow to cool.

4   Reheat the remaining soup in the pot on High for about 15 minutes until piping hot or quickly reheat in a saucepan on the hob. Season to taste with salt and pepper and served in a warm bowl accompanied by crusty wholemeal bread.

Second serving

• Either cover the cooled soup and chill in the fridge for the following day, or freeze for up to a month. If frozen, allow the soup to defrost in the fridge overnight. To serve, transfer to a saucepan and heat until piping hot.

Cook's tips

• Try spicing up the second serving by stirring in 5 ml/1 tsp of curry paste when heating (whisk well to make sure it's blended) or adding a pinch of crushed dried chilli flakes. Serve with mini popadoms or tortilla chips.
• For a thinner soup, stir in a little extra hot stock or milk before serving.

light meals

All the recipes in this book are quick and easy to prepare, but in this chapter you'll find some of the simplest ones designed for those days when you've already had a main meal or just want a light lunch or supper dish.

You'll find a wide choice of light meals here to suit all tastes, from familiar dishes such as Macaroni Cheese (see pages 44–5) and Creamy Chicken Pâté (see pages 50–51) to more unusual ones including Harissa-spiced Chick Peas (see pages 54–5) and Grilled Vegetable Bake (see pages 52–3). There's plenty of scope for vegetarians as well, with many of the recipes in this chapter being meat-free.

Plus, don't forget all the delicious soups in the previous chapter, which are perfect for a light meal.

Light meals tips

- It's worth making larger quantities of pâtés and freezing in individual portions, well wrapped, so you can use them over the following few weeks.

- If you use crème fraîche, always use the full-fat variety. Recipes that include crème fraîche are Macaroni Cheese (see pages 44–5), Creamy Chicken Pâté (sees pages 50–51) and Normandy Chicken (see pages 158–9).

- Any of the recipes are easily doubled so you can serve the second portion the following day.

- Always add dried herbs at the start of cooking and fresh herbs towards the end of cooking.

- There are so many delicious flavoured and plain breads you can serve to accompany your meals, you need never run out of ideas.

- Ready-made salad bags are expensive but avoid waste when you are cooking for one. Do make sure you re-seal the bag tightly once opened – using a clip-it is best. A little air in the bag also helps to keep the salad fresher.

macaroni cheese

Chef's note

A great storecupboard standby, this well-known dish is traditionally made with a flour-thickened cheese sauce. In this modern version, macaroni is combined with crème fraîche and stock and as the pasta cooks it soaks up the liquid to create a delicious sauce.

V

Suitable for Vegetarians

150 ml/¼ pint/⅔ cup **crème fraîche**

200 ml/7 fl oz/scant 1 cup boiling **vegetable stock**

50 g/2 oz **easy-cook macaroni**

Salt and freshly ground black pepper

1   Put the crème fraîche in the ceramic cooking pot, then whisk in the stock a little at a time. Switch on the slow cooker to High.

2   Add the macaroni, season with salt and pepper and give the mixture a stir. Cover with the lid and cook for ¾–1 hour or until the pasta is cooked and the sauce is thick and creamy.

3   Spoon the pasta and sauce on to a warm serving plate or bowl and serve straight away sprinkled with grated Cheddar or Parmesan. Serve with a mixed green salad.

Cook's tips

- It's important to use full-fat crème fraîche for this recipe as low- and half-fat versions tend to separate when heated. If you want to reduce the amount of fat a little, use 100 ml/3½ fl oz/scant ½ cup of crème fraîche and 250 ml/8 fl oz/1 cup of stock, then serve with just a small amount of grated cheese.
- Vary the recipe by adding a few snipped sun-dried tomatoes to the stock (you'll need to add an extra spoonful of stock as these soak up liquid), or stir in some thawed frozen peas and sweetcorn or fresh or frozen chopped herbs such as parsley or coriander (cilantro) towards the end of cooking.

boston baked beans

2

3-4 hrs **LOW**

Warm crusty bread or a jacket potato

1 small **red onion**, finely chopped, or 25 g/1 oz **frozen diced onion**

100 ml/3½ fl oz/scant ½ cup hot (not boiling) **vegetable stock**

1 **whole clove** (optional)

1 **bay leaf**

400 g/14 oz/large can of **cannellini beans**

15 ml/1 tbsp **tomato ketchup** (catsup)

7.5 ml/1½ tsp **black treacle** (molasses)

7.5 ml/1½ tsp **dark brown sugar**

5 ml/1 tsp **Dijon mustard**

12 cooked **mini pork sausages**

Salt and freshly ground black pepper

1   Put the onion in the ceramic cooking pot and pour over about half the stock. Add the clove, if using, and the bay leaf. Cover with the lid and switch on the slow cooker to Low. Leave to warm for a few minutes while measuring and preparing the rest of the ingredients.

2   Tip the beans into a sieve (strainer) and rinse under cold running water. Drain thoroughly. Stir the ketchup, treacle, sugar and mustard into the remaining stock until blended.

3   Put the beans in a layer on top of the onions, top with the sausages, then pour the stock mixture over. Re-cover with the lid and cook for 3–4 hours or until the onions are tender. Season to taste with salt and pepper.

4   Spoon half the Boston baked beans into a bowl or freezer container and allow to cool. Serve the remainder at once with warm crusty bread or a jacket potato.

Second serving

- Either cover the cooled Boston baked beans and chill in the fridge for the following day, or freeze for up to a month. If frozen, allow to defrost in the fridge overnight. To serve, gently heat in a saucepan with an extra tablespoonful of stock or water, bubbling for a few minutes to ensure that the sausages and beans are piping hot.

Cook's tips

- Black treacle gives the beans a rich flavour and dark colour, but you can use maple syrup instead, if you prefer.
- For a vegetarian version, leave out the sausages and serve sprinkled with grated cheese.

savoury chicken and rice

1

1 hr
HIGH

Complete meal
in itself

Chef's note

This is a great way to use bought ready-cooked or leftover chicken – and also pork or beef. You could double the ingredients for the rice and use the second portion to serve with a dish from the freezer the next day.

4 **spring onions** (scallions), sliced

200 g/7 oz/small can of **chopped tomatoes**

175 ml/6 fl oz/¾ cup boiling **chicken** or **vegetable stock**

½ red (bell) **pepper**, seeded and chopped, or 50 g/2 oz **frozen sliced mixed peppers**

A pinch of **dried mixed herbs**

75 g/3 oz/⅓ cup **easy-cook (converted) rice**

Salt and freshly ground black pepper

75 g/3 oz/¾ cup roughly chopped **cooked chicken**

1   Put the spring onions in the ceramic cooking pot. Pour the tomatoes over, then the stock. Cover with the lid and switch on the slow cooker to High. Leave for a few minutes while measuring and preparing the rest of the ingredients.

2   Stir in the chopped pepper and the herbs, then sprinkle the rice over. Season with salt and pepper and stir again.

3   Re-cover with the lid and cook for 50–60 minutes or until the rice is just tender and has absorbed most of the liquid.

4   Stir in the chicken and cook for a further 10 minutes to heat the chicken through before serving.

Cook's tips

- If you prefer, instead of adding cooked chicken at the end of cooking, stir 100 g/4 oz of raw chicken breast, cut into 2.5 cm/1 in cubes, with the peppers.
- A small can of drained and flaked tuna fish or salmon also work well in this dish instead of the meat.
- You can also stir in some chopped fresh herbs with the chicken, if liked, for extra flavour.

creamy chicken pâté

3-4

2½-3 hrs
HIGH

Melba toast or
French bread

Chef's note

If you have a food
processor, this rich,
buttery pâté can be made
in just a few minutes and
then left to cook while
you get on with the rest of
your day. It makes an
excellent lunch with
bread and salad and will
keep for several days in
the fridge.

25 g/1 oz/2 tbsp softened **butter**,
plus extra for greasing

½ small **onion** or 1 **shallot**,
chopped, or 15 g/½ oz **frozen
diced onion**

15 ml/1 tbsp **sherry** or **brandy**

1 **egg**

225 g/8 oz **chicken livers**

1 skinless, boneless **chicken
breast**, about 175 g/6 oz

30 ml/2 tbsp **crème fraîche** or
double (heavy) cream

2.5 ml/½ tsp **dried thyme** or
mixed herbs

**Salt and freshly ground black
pepper**

1. Lightly grease a 600 ml/1 pint/2½ cup terrine or heatproof dish (first make sure that it will fit in the ceramic cooking pot) and line with non-stick baking parchment. Place an upturned saucer or metal pastry (paste) cutter in the bottom of the pot. Pour in about 2.5 cm/1 in of very hot (not boiling) water, then turn on the slow cooker to High.

2. Put the onion or shallot in a food processor with the sherry or brandy. Break in the egg and process for about 1 minute or until the onion is finely chopped.

3. Roughly chop the chicken livers, removing any discoloured pieces or stringy bits, and add to the food processor. Chop the chicken breast into small pieces, then add to the food processor with the butter. Process until fairly smooth, then add the crème fraîche or cream and the herbs. Season with salt and pepper. Process briefly again until mixed.

4. Spoon the pâté mixture into the prepared dish and level the top. Cover with clingfilm (plastic wrap) or lightly greased foil, then place in the pot and pour in enough boiling water to come two-thirds of the way up the dish. Cook for 2½–3 hours or until firm in the centre.

5. Carefully remove the dish from the pot and place on a wire cooling rack. When cool, chill in the fridge for at least 2 hours.

6. Run a palette knife around the edge of the dish and turn out the pâté. Remove the lining paper and cut the pâté into portions. Serve with melba toast or French bread.

Remaining servings

• Wrap each portion in clingfilm or foil and either keep chilled in the fridge for up to 3 days or freeze for up to a month. If frozen, defrost in the fridge for several hours or overnight.

grilled vegetable bake

1

2-4 hrs
AUTO

Ciabatta or
focaccia bread

Chef's note

Frozen grilled (broiled)
vegetables – a mix of
grilled red and yellow
(bell) peppers,
courgettes (zucchini) and
aubergines (eggplant) –
are a brilliant buy as they
need no further
preparation. Here they
are combined with
almonds in a savoury
lightly set custard – a bit
like quiche but without
the pastry!

V

Suitable for
Vegetarians

A little softened **butter** or
sunflower oil for greasing

175 g/6 oz **frozen grilled
vegetables**, preferably thawed

1 **egg**

1.5 ml/¼ tsp **Dijon mustard**

150 ml/¼ pint/⅔ cup **milk**

30 ml/2 tbsp **ground almonds**

15 ml/1 tbsp fresh **white
breadcrumbs**

50 g/2 oz/½ cup grated **Gruyère
cheese**

**Salt and freshly ground black
pepper**

25 g/1 oz/¼ cup **flaked
(slivered) almonds**

1   Place an upturned saucer or a metal pastry (paste) cutter in the base of the ceramic cooking pot. Pour in about 5 cm/2 in of very hot (not boiling) water, then turn on the slow cooker to Auto. Grease a 13–15 cm/5–6 in round heatproof dish with the butter or oil.

2   Put the vegetables in the dish. Whisk together the egg and mustard, then stir in the milk, ground almonds, breadcrumbs and cheese. Season with salt and pepper, then pour carefully over the vegetables.

3   Let the mixture settle for about a minute, then sprinkle the almonds over the top. Cover the dish with clingfilm (plastic wrap) or lightly greased foil and place on top of the saucer or pastry cutter in the pot. Pour in enough boiling water to come half-way up the side of the dish or tin.

4   Cover with the lid and cook for 2–4 hours or until the vegetables are very tender and the mixture is lightly set (check this by pushing a thin knife or skewer into the middle – it should feel hot and there should be little liquid). Serve hot with ciabatta or focaccia bread.

Cook's tips

- Frozen grilled vegetables are also used to make Red Lentil and Vegetable Dhal (see pages 210–11).
- For a browned top, place under a moderate grill (broiler) for about a minute until golden brown. Watch carefully, as the almonds will brown very quickly.

harissa-spiced chick peas

1

2-3 hrs
LOW

Complete meal in itself

4 **spring onions** (scallions), trimmed and sliced

1 small **garlic clove**, crushed, or 2.5 ml/½ tsp **garlic purée** (paste)

5 ml/1 tsp **harissa paste**

30 ml/2 tbsp hot (not boiling) **vegetable stock** or **water**

½ × 400 g/14 oz/large can of **chick peas** (garbanzos), drained and rinsed

200 g/7 oz/small can of **chopped tomatoes with herbs**

50 g/2 oz fresh **baby spinach leaves** or 25 g/1 oz defrosted **frozen spinach**

75 g/3 oz **Halloumi cheese**, cut into small cubes

Salt and freshly ground black pepper

1   Put the spring onions, garlic and harissa paste in the ceramic cooking pot. Add the stock or water and stir until blended, then stir in the chick peas and tomatoes.

2   Cover with the lid and switch on the slow cooker to Low. Cook for 1½–2½ hours or until the spring onions are tender.

3   Place the spinach leaves on top of the mixture so that they will cook in the steam and increase the temperature to High. Re-cover with the lid and cook for a further 30 minutes or until the spinach is tender.

4   Stir the spinach and the Halloumi cheese into the mixture. Season to taste with salt and freshly ground black pepper. Spoon on to a warm plate and serve straight away as the cheese begins to soften.

Cook's tips

- Harissa is a fiery chilli paste, popular in North African cuisine. It comes in small 75 g/3 oz jars and can be found alongside other jars of spice. Once opened, refrigerate and use within 6 weeks.
- If preferred, substitute a can of mixed, borlotti or kidney beans for the chick peas.
- Chick peas are also used to make Chicken Masala Soup (see pages 36–7).

cheesy bread pudding

1

2-4 hrs
LOW

A tomato or
green salad

Chef's note

When your kitchen caters for just one, the last few slices of bread in the loaf often become stale and this simple homely dish is a great way to use them up. Chunks of buttered bread cooked in a cheese-flavoured savoury custard is comfort food at its best!

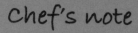

V

Suitable for
vegetarians

1   Place an upturned saucer or a metal pastry (paste) cutter in the base of the ceramic cooking pot and pour in 2.5 cm/1 in of very hot (not boiling) water. Switch on to Auto or Low.

2   Cut the bread into small cubes about 1 cm/½ in square.

3   Lightly beat the egg in a mixing bowl, then stir in the milk and season with a little salt and pepper. Add the bread cubes and leave to soak for 5 minutes while measuring and preparing the rest of the ingredients.

4   Thickly grease the base and sides of a 600 ml/1 pint/2½ cup heatproof dish about 5 cm/2 in deep (make sure first that it fits inside the ceramic cooking pot). Add about half of the cheese to the soaked bread mixture and stir gently to combine. Tip into the prepared dish.

5   Sprinkle the rest of the cheese over the top and cover the dish with clingfilm (plastic wrap) or foil.

6   Place the dish on top of the saucer or pastry cutter in the pot, then pour in enough boiling water to come half-way up the dish. Cover with the lid and cook for 2–4 hours or until the custard is lightly set.

7   Carefully remove the dish from the pot and serve the cheesy bread pudding hot with a tomato or green salad.

Cook's tips

- For a browned top place under a moderate grill (broiler) until puffed up and golden brown.
- For a chilli tomato cheese and bread pudding, add a pinch of crushed dried chilli flakes and use either sun-dried tomato flavoured bread or add 25 g/1 oz of finely chopped sun-dried tomatoes when soaking the bread.

mixed fish terrine

2-3

3 hrs HIGH

15 ml/1 tbsp crème fraiche mixed with chopped dill

Chef's note

A combination of firm white fish and pretty pink salmon gives this dish an attractive marbled effect when sliced. Even though the terrine is so simple to make, it makes a very special lunch or main course to serve on a hot summer's day.

5 ml/1 tsp **sunflower oil**

150 g/5 oz **smoked salmon** or **smoked trout**

400 g/14 oz skinned boneless firm **white fish** such as haddock, cod or whiting

1 **egg**, lightly beaten

60 ml/4 tbsp **crème fraîche** or **double (heavy) cream**

5 ml/1 tsp **Dijon mustard**

5 ml/1 tsp finely grated **lemon zest** (optional)

Salt and white pepper

1   Pour about 2.5 cm/1 in hot (not boiling) water into the ceramic cooking pot and switch on the slow cooker to High. Lightly grease a 450 ml/¾ pt/2 cup loaf tin or a dish with the oil.

2   Use about two-thirds of the smoked salmon or smoked trout to line the tin or dish, allowing some of the pieces to hang over the edge. Cut the rest into strips about 5 cm/2 in long. Cut the white fish into strips of a similar length.

3   Mix together the egg, crème fraîche or cream, mustard and lemon zest, if using, in a bowl. Season with salt and pepper, then stir in the strips of fish.

4   Spoon the fish mixture into the tin or dish and smooth the surface level. Fold the overhanging pieces of salmon over the mixture. Cover tightly with clingfilm (plastic wrap) or foil.

5   Place in the cooking pot and pour in enough boiling water to come just over half-way up the sides of the tin or dish. Cover with the lid and cook on High for 3 hours or until the terrine is lightly set and a skewer inserted into the middle comes out clean.

6   Carefully remove from the slow cooker and place on a wire cooling rack. When cool, chill in the fridge for at least 2 hours before turning out and slicing.

7   Serve with crème fraîche and chopped fresh dill.

Second serving

• The terrine will keep in the fridge for a day. It's good served with a mixed salad or hot buttered new potatoes and a green vegetable.

seafood

Succulent and delicious, fish is eminently suitable for the slow cooker as the gentle, even cooking ensures that it retains its shape and doesn't disintegrate during cooking. Although large whole fish won't fit in the slow cooker, it's absolutely perfect for single-portion fish steaks and fillets.

Fish is a great source of protein and provides many vitamins and minerals. White fish is particularly low in fat, making it the perfect food for helping to maintain a healthy weight. Ideally, you should eat oily fish such as salmon and tuna at least once a week as it contains beneficial heart-healthy fats.

Unlike meat, fish cooks relatively quickly in the slow cooker, taking about the same time as rice and pasta, so it is superb for combining with these easy-to-make all-in-one meals. Here you'll find wonderful fresh fish dishes such as Spicy Salmon Steak (see pages 68–9) and Braised Turbot in White Wine (see pages 80–1), as well as a good selection of recipes for convenient canned fish, including Crab and Corn Chowder (see pages 64–5) and Tuna Cannelloni (see pages 76–7).

seafood tips

- When buying fish, remember that if it's really fresh it shouldn't smell 'fishy'. Obviously, it's difficult to test pre-packed fish for freshness, but buy from a reliable source and make sure that it looks firm and moist.

- When you open pre-packed fish, check that there is no smell of ammonia. If there is, the fish is off.

- Both fresh and frozen seafood should be put in the fridge or freezer as soon as possible and, ideally, fresh fish should be cooked and eaten on the day you buy it.

- You can use stock, water or wine to cook fish and will only need small quantities of liquid.

- If you thicken with cream, milk or egg yolks, add them for the final 30 minutes.

- Types of firm-fleshed white fish are interchangeable in recipes.

- Only season lightly if you are using smoked fish.

smoked haddock kedgeree

1

1-1¼ hrs
HIGH

Fingers of hot buttered toast

A little softened **butter** for greasing

250 ml/8 fl oz/1 cup hot (not boiling) **vegetable stock**

75 g/3 oz/⅓ cup **easy-cook (converted) rice**

5 ml/1 tsp **curry powder**

Salt and freshly ground black pepper

100 g/4 oz **smoked haddock fillet**, skinned

5 ml/1 tsp **lemon juice**

15 ml/1 tbsp fresh or frozen **chopped chives, coriander** (cilantro) or **parsley**

1 hard-boiled (hard-cooked) **egg**, quartered (optional)

1   Grease the base of the ceramic cooking pot with the butter, then pour in the stock.

2   Add the rice and curry powder, stir well and season with a little salt and pepper. Cover with the lid and switch on the slow cooker to High. Cook for 45 minutes.

3   Meanwhile, cut the fish into bite-sized pieces. Sprinkle the lemon juice over, then stir into the rice.

4   Cook for a further 15–20 minutes or until the rice and fish are cooked and most of the stock has been absorbed.

5   Stir in most of the chopped herbs and spoon on to a warm serving plate. Sprinkle with the remaining herbs and top with the egg quarters, if using. Serve with fingers of hot buttered toast.

Cook's tip

• When buying smoked haddock, look for the natural pale golden un-dyed fillets as they have a better flavour than the bright yellow fish, which are artificially coloured. The smoked haddock can be replaced with fresh haddock or fresh salmon, if you prefer.

crab and corn chowder

1

2½ hrs LOW

Warm crusty bread

4 **spring onions** (scallions), trimmed and thinly sliced

1 **celery stick**, finely chopped

150 ml/¼ pint/⅔ cup very hot (not boiling) **vegetable** or **fish stock**

1 **potato**, about 200 g/7 oz, cut into chunks

50 g/2 oz **frozen mixed vegetables**

100 g/4 oz/4 tbsp **frozen sweetcorn** or ½ × 200 g/7 oz/small can of **sweetcorn**, drained

100 ml/3½ fl oz/scant ½ cup **milk**

150 g/5 oz fresh **white crabmeat** or a 175 g/6 oz can of **white crabmeat in brine**, drained

15 ml/1 tbsp fresh or frozen chopped **parsley**

Salt and freshly ground black pepper

15 ml/1 tbsp **crème fraîche** or **natural thick yoghurt**

1   Put the spring onions and celery in the ceramic cooking pot.

2   Pour the stock over, cover with the lid and switch on the slow cooker to Low. Leave for a few minutes while measuring and preparing the rest of the ingredients.

3   Add the potato and mixed vegetables to the pot. Re-cover with the lid and cook for 2 hours or until the vegetables are tender.

4   Stir in the sweetcorn, milk, crabmeat and most of the parsley. Cook for a further 30 minutes or until the chowder is piping hot.

5   Season to taste with salt and pepper, then ladle into a warm bowl and top with a swirl of crème fraîche or yoghurt and sprinkle the rest of the parsley over. Serve with warm crusty bread.

Cook's tip
• If using canned crabmeat, take care when adding salt to the soup as the crabmeat is preserved in brine, so will already be quite salty.

salmon and dill mousse

1

1 - 1½ hrs
LOW

A green salad
and brown bread
and butter

Chef's note

Using both smoked and
fresh salmon, these
individual mousses make
a great supper dish or are
perfect served as a
starter when entertaining.
Inexpensive smoked
salmon trimmings are
ideal for this recipe.

50 g/2 oz skinned fresh **salmon**

150 g/5 oz thinly sliced **smoked
salmon**

1 **egg yolk**

45 ml/3 tbsp **double (heavy)
cream**

25 g/1 oz/2 tbsp **cream cheese**

5 ml/1 tsp **lemon juice**

**Salt and freshly ground black
pepper**

5 ml/1 tsp fresh or frozen
chopped **dill** (dill weed) or
parsley

1   Pour about 2 cm/¾ in of very hot (not boiling) water into the base of the ceramic cooking pot and switch on the slow cooker to Low.

2   Roughly chop the fresh salmon and 25 g/1 oz of the smoked salmon and put in a food processor. Process for a few seconds until finely chopped, then add the egg yolk, cream, cream cheese, lemon juice and salt and pepper. Process again until everything is mixed together and the mixture is fairly smooth. Add the dill or parsley and process for just a few seconds until evenly mixed.

3   Line two 150 ml/¼ pint/⅔ cup ramekins (custard cups) with about three-quarters of the remaining smoked salmon. Spoon in the mousse mixture, then cover with the remaining smoked salmon.

4   Cover the ramekins with clingfilm (plastic wrap) or lightly greased foil and put them in the slow cooker. Pour in enough boiling water to come half-way up the sides of the dishes. Cover with the lid and cook for 1–1½ hours or until the mousses are just set and firm to the touch. Carefully remove from the water and leave to cool. Turn out one of the mousses and chill until ready to serve. Accompany with a green salad and brown bread and butter or hot buttered toast.

Second serving
• Chill the second salmon mousse in the fridge for up to 2 days. Turn out and serve as before. This mousse is not suitable for freezing.

Cook's tip
• You could use chopped parsley instead if the dill, if preferred.

spicy salmon steak

1

1¼ hrs
LOW

Rice or warmed
naan bread

Chef's note

This mild fish curry is wonderfully fragrant and the creamy coconut sauce is an excellent way to cook salmon, keeping it moist and succulent. Serve on a bed of steamed rice or simply accompany with some warmed naan bread.

25 g/1 oz **creamed coconut**, roughly chopped

150 ml/¼ pint/⅔ cup hot (not boiling) **vegetable stock**

4 **spring onions** (scallions), trimmed and finely sliced

5 ml/1 tsp grated fresh **root ginger** or **bottled ginger**

10 ml/2 tsp **korma** or other **mild curry paste**

150 g/5 oz skinned **salmon steak**

Salt and freshly ground black pepper

1   Put the creamed coconut in the ceramic cooking pot. Pour in the stock and stir until the coconut has dissolved. Add the spring onions, ginger and curry paste and stir again until blended.

2   Lightly season the salmon with salt and pepper. Add to the pot, cover with the lid and switch on the slow cooker to High or Low. Cook for ¾ hour on High or 1–1¼ hours on Low or until the salmon is just cooked.

3   Carefully remove the salmon from the slow cooker and serve on a warm plate with the sauce spooned over. Accompany the salmon with boiled or steamed rice or warmed naan bread.

Cook's tips

- You could stir a tablespoonful of fresh or frozen chopped coriander (cilantro) into the sauce before serving.
- Creamed coconut is sold in blocks and is a useful ingredient as it can be chopped and mixed with hot stock or water to make the required amount of coconut milk. It will keep for several months in the fridge.
- Spring onions are a great buy when you're cooking for one, as ordinary onions are often too large when preparing small quantities of food. Keep them in a paper or an open plastic bag (to allow air to circulate) in the salad drawer in the fridge.

luxury fish pie

Chef's note

A layer of ready-made or leftover cooked mashed potato helps to seal in all the juices from the fish and prawns as they cook. The filling has the simplest of sauces, made by mixing herby cream cheese with milk.

1

1 hr
HIGH

A mixed green salad

150 g/5 oz fresh or smoked **haddock fillet**, skinned

50 g/2 oz shelled raw **prawns** (shrimp), halved if large

7.5 ml/1½ tsp **cornflour** (cornstarch)

25 g/1 oz/1 tbsp **frozen sweetcorn**

25 g/1 oz/1 tbsp **frozen peas**

50 g/2 oz/¼ cup full-fat plain **cream cheese** or **cream cheese with garlic and herbs**

45 ml/3 tbsp **milk**

Salt and freshly ground black pepper

225 g/8 oz cold **mashed potato** or ½ × 400 g/14 oz packet of **ready-made mashed potato**

1   Cut the haddock into bite-sized pieces and place in a bowl with the prawns. Sprinkle the cornflour over and toss to coat. Add the sweetcorn and peas.

2   Blend together the cream cheese and milk and a little salt and pepper. Pour over the fish and vegetables (this mixture will be very thick but will be diluted with the juices from the fish as it cooks) and gently mix together. Spoon into the ceramic cooking pot and switch on the slow cooker to High.

3   Give the mashed potatoes a brief stir to soften, then spoon on top of the fish mixture in an even layer. Cover with the lid and switch on to High. Cook for 1 hour or until the fish is cooked. Serve straight away with a mixed green salad.

Cook's tips

- Brown the potato topping under a moderate grill (broiler) before serving, if liked.
- Try hake, fresh tuna, salmon or cod instead of the haddock for a change.

cod with onions and capers

1

**1 - 1¼ hrs
LOW**

Mashed or new potatoes and a green vegetable

Chef's note

When made with the freshest fish, this simple supper is a real winner and a trouble-free way to cook cod or other white fish. The richness of caramelised onions is offset with a dash of white wine and a few capers, which have a sharp citrus flavour.

½ × 400 g/14 oz/large can of **fried onions in olive oil**

90 ml/6 tbsp **white wine** or **vegetable stock** or a combination of both

15 g/½ oz/1 tbsp **butter**, softened

10 ml/2 tsp **capers**, drained and chopped

15 ml/1 tbsp fresh or frozen chopped **coriander** (cilantro) or **parsley**

Salt and freshly ground black pepper

150 g/5 oz thick **cod fillet**

1   Put the onions in the ceramic cooking pot and spoon the stock over. Blend the butter with the capers, coriander or parsley and a little salt and pepper.

2   Place the fish on top of the onions and dot the top with the flavoured butter. Cover with the lid and switch on the slow cooker to High. Cook for 1–1¼ hours or until the fish is just cooked; it should be opaque and flake easily.

3   To serve, spoon the fish and onions on to a warm serving plate. Serve with creamy mashed potatoes or boiled new potatoes and a green vegetable.

Cook's tips

- Any firm fish fillet may be used instead of the cod in this dish. Try halibut, hake, swordfish, haddock or salmon for a change.
- Capers are the flower buds of a bush native to the Mediterranean. The buds are picked when firm and unopened and preserved in vinegar and salt, so take care not to over-season the flavoured butter. Chopped olives and a dash of lemon juice or vinegar make a good alternative to the capers.

fresh swordfish with lentils

 **1**

 **3½ hrs HIGH**

Complete meal in itself

Chef's note

Puy lentils are dark green in colour and have a unique peppery flavour. They retain their shape even after long, slow cooking, which makes them perfect for this dish. You'll find them in any major supermarket.

15 ml/1 tbsp **frozen diced onions**

1 **fennel bulb**, thinly sliced

1 **garlic clove**, crushed or 5 ml/1 tsp **garlic purée** (paste)

5 ml/1 tsp **chilli flakes**

A small pinch of **fennel seeds** (optional)

A small pinch of **dried mixed herbs**

50 g/2 oz/⅓ cup **puy lentils**, rinsed

250 ml/8 fl oz/1 cup hot (not boiling) **vegetable stock**

150 g/5 oz **swordfish steak**

5 ml/1 tsp **oil**

Salt and freshly ground black pepper

1   Put the onion, fennel, garlic, chilli, fennel seeds, if using, and herbs in the ceramic cooking pot. Stir in the lentils and stock and cover with the lid.

2   Turn on the slow cooker to High and cook for 2½ hours or until the lentils are just tender.

3   Brush both sides of the swordfish with the oil. Season the lentil mixture with salt and pepper and stir. Place the swordfish on top, re-cover and cook for 1 hour or until the fish and lentils are cooked through.

Cook's tip

• Double the quantity of lentil and vegetable mixture and remove half before adding the fish at step 3. Serve the following day as a salad drizzled with a little French dressing and scattered with crumbled Feta.

tuna cannelloni

Chef's note

This all-in-one dish makes the most of storecupboard ingredients, such as canned tuna and tomatoes, so is ideal for those days when you haven't had time to shop. A mixed green salad makes a great accompaniment.

1

2-2½ hrs HIGH

A mixed green salad

A little **olive oil** for greasing

200 g/7 oz/small can of **tuna in oil**, drained

200 g/7 oz/small can of **chopped tomatoes with herbs**

25 g/1 oz/½ cup fresh **white breadcrumbs**

25 g/1 oz/1 tbsp **frozen peas**

Salt and freshly ground black pepper

5 **cannelloni** tubes

For the topping:

25 g/1 oz/¼ cup grated **mature Cheddar cheese** or 15 g/½ oz/ 2 tbsp grated **Parmesan cheese**

½ × 400 g/14 oz jar of **white sauce**

1   Grease the base and about a third of the way up the ceramic cooking pot with oil.

2   Tip the tuna into a bowl and break into large flakes with a fork. Add the tomatoes, breadcrumbs and peas. Season generously with salt and pepper, then mix together. Use the mixture to fill the cannelloni tubes. Arrange the cannelloni tubes on the base of the pot, preferably in a single layer.

3   Stir about half of the cheese into the white sauce, then spoon over the cannelloni, smoothing the top level with the back of the spoon. Sprinkle the remaining cheese over the top.

4   Cover with the lid and switch on the slow cooker to Auto or High. Cook for 1 hour, then leave on Auto or reduce the temperature to Low and cook for a further 1–1½ hours or until the cannelloni is tender. Serve at once with a mixed green salad.

Cook's tips

- White sauce is also used for Easy Vegetable Lasagne (see pages 214–15). Alternatively, make your own white sauce (also on page 215).
- A small can of salmon, sardines or white crabmeat makes a great alternative to the tuna.
- For a browned top, sprinkle a little extra grated cheese over and place under a moderate grill (broiler) until golden brown and bubbling.

easy salmon risotto

2

1³⁄₄ hrs HIGH

Ciabatta bread

Chef's note

Making risotto on the hob can be tedious as you need to add the liquid bit by bit and stir constantly. In the slow cooker, it can be added all at once, then left to cook in the gentle heat with little attention.

20 g/³⁄₄ oz/1½ tbsp **butter**

4 **spring onions** (scallions), trimmed and finely sliced

50 g/2 oz/¼ cup **easy-cook (converted) Italian risotto rice**

30 ml/2 tbsp **white wine** or **extra stock**

175 ml/6 fl oz/³⁄₄ cup hot (not boiling) **vegetable stock**

150 g/5 oz **salmon fillet**, cut into bite-sized pieces

Salt and freshly ground black pepper

15 ml/1 tbsp chopped **fresh dill** (dill weed)

Freshly grated **Parmesan cheese**

A sprig of **fresh dill**

1   Put the butter in the ceramic cooking pot and switch on the slow cooker to High. In about 10–15 minutes, when it has melted, stir in the spring onions, cover with the lid and cook for 30 minutes.

2   Add the rice and stir to coat in the butter, then stir in the wine, if using. Add the stock, stir, then re-cover and cook for 40 minutes, stirring once half-way through the cooking time.

3   Season the salmon pieces with salt and pepper and stir into the rice. Cook for a further 20 minutes or until the salmon is opaque and the rice is tender.

4   Stir in the chopped dill, then switch off the slow cooker and leave the risotto to stand for a minute.

5   Gently stir, then spoon on to a warmed plate or bowl and sprinkle with some grated Parmesan. Garnish with a sprig of fresh dill and serve at once with Ciabatta bread.

Cook's tip

• Strips of smoked salmon and cooked, peeled prawns (shrimp) can be used instead of fresh salmon. Stir these in about 10 minutes before the end of cooking.

braised turbot in white wine

1

2-2½ hrs
LOW

French bread

Chef's note

This fragrant dish has a real Mediterranean feel and flavour. Cooked with herbs, orange and a dash of white wine, it relies on good-quality fresh fish. Serve simply with plenty of crusty French bread.

4 **spring onions** (scallions), trimmed and finely sliced

1 **garlic clove**, crushed, or 2.5 ml/½ tsp **garlic purée** (paste)

A sprig of **fresh thyme** or a small pinch of **dried thyme**

1 **bay leaf**

A thinly pared strip of **orange peel**

45 ml/3 tbsp **white wine**

About 150 g/5 oz of **turbot fillet**, skinned

Salt and freshly ground black pepper

45 ml/3 tbsp fresh **orange juice**

1 **tomato**, sliced

3–5 stoned (pitted) **black olives**

Opposite: Braised Turbot in White Wine (see above)

1   Put the spring onions, garlic, thyme, bay leaf and orange peel in the ceramic cooking pot. Pour the wine over, cover with the lid and switch on the slow cooker to Low.

2   Lightly season the fish with salt and pepper, then place on top of the onion mixture. Drizzle the orange juice over, then arrange the tomato slices on top and scatter the olives around the sides.

3   Re-cover with the lid and cook for 2–2½ hours or until the fish is opaque and flakes easily. Transfer to a warm plate, discard the orange peel and bay leaf and serve at once with warm crusty French bread.

Cook's tips

• For a more substantial dish, add a 200 g/7 oz/small can of artichoke hearts, drained and cut into quarters, with the olives.
• Don't worry if the fish isn't completely submerged in the liquid. It cooks by a combination of braising and steaming.
• If you don't want to buy a whole bottle of wine just for this dish, look out for 'taster' bottles and small cans of wine. Always choose a wine that you'd also enjoy drinking as very cheap 'cooking' wines often spoil the flavour of a dish.

Opposite: Chilli Baked Beans (see pages 198–99)

simple seafood paella

 **1**

 **2 hrs HIGH**

 **Complete meal in itself**

Chef's note

Ready-prepared seafood can be bought in small quantities from most supermarket delicatessen counters or from the chilled or freezer section, which is so useful if you're cooking for one. If you buy frozen, allow the seafood to defrost thoroughly in the fridge.

15 ml/1 tbsp **frozen diced onion**

½ red (bell) **pepper**, seeded and chopped

1 **garlic clove**, crushed or 5 ml/1 tsp **garlic purée** (paste)

A pinch of **dried mixed herbs**

A pinch of **ground turmeric**

200 g/7 oz/small can of **chopped tomatoes**

175 ml/6 fl oz/¾ cup hot (not boiling) **vegetable stock**

75 g/3 oz/⅓ cup **easy-cook (converted) rice**

Salt and freshly ground black pepper

100 g/4 oz **mixed cooked seafood** (prawns, mussels and squid rings)

1 Stir together the onion, pepper, garlic, herbs and turmeric in the ceramic cooking pot. Add the tomatoes and stock. Cover with the lid, switch on the slow cooker to High and cook for 1½ hours.

2 Sprinkle the rice over the tomato mixture and season with salt and pepper. Stir, then re-cover and cook for 45 minutes.

3 Stir in the seafood and cook for a further 15 minutes until the rice is tender and most of the liquid has been absorbed.

Cook's tip
• Snip your fresh herbs with scissors, then freeze. You can then use them straight from the freezer.

king prawn and spinach balti

1

2-4 hrs
LOW

Naan bread

Chef's note

This easy curry with large juicy prawns has a spicy kick. The sauce is slowly simmered for several hours, then the prawns added for the last few minutes so they are cooked but not toughened. The term 'balti' refers to the steel or iron pot in which the food is usually cooked, but a slow cooker works just as well!

25 g/1 oz **creamed coconut**, chopped

150 ml/¼ pint/⅔ cup hot (not boiling) **vegetable stock**

10 ml/2 tsp **balti curry paste**

1 small **garlic clove**, crushed, or 2.5 ml/½ tsp **garlic purée** (paste)

1.5 ml/¼ tsp **red chilli paste** (optional)

1 small **onion**, finely chopped, or 25 g/1 oz **frozen diced onion**

25 g/1 oz roughly chopped fresh or frozen cooked **spinach**

6 large peeled **raw tiger prawns** (jumbo shrimp)

15 ml/1 tbsp fresh or frozen chopped **coriander** (cilantro)

Salt and freshly ground black pepper

1 Put the creamed coconut in the ceramic cooking pot. Add the stock and stir until the coconut has dissolved.

2 Stir in the curry paste, garlic and chilli paste, if using, until blended. Add the onion, cover with the lid and switch on the slow cooker to Low. Cook for 2–3 hours or until the onion is very tender.

3 Meanwhile, if using frozen spinach, put it in a sieve (strainer) over a bowl and leave to defrost and drain at room temperature. Stir the thawed or fresh spinach into the curry mixture with the prawns and most of the coriander. Cook for a further 15–20 minutes or until the prawns are tender and completely pink.

4 Taste and season with salt and pepper. Serve in a warm bowl with the remaining coriander sprinkled over. Balti is traditionally served without a knife and fork; torn pieces of warmed naan bread are used to scoop up the curry.

Cook's tips

- Balti curry paste contains lots of spices and seasonings, including tomato purée, coriander, turmeric, cumin, ginger, tamarind, lemon juice, chilli, creamed coconut and parsley.
- If you like the flavour of garlic, it's worth buying a tube of garlic purée, which will save on preparation time. About 5 ml/1 tsp is the equivalent of a large garlic clove. Once opened, it will keep in the fridge for about 3 months. Gentle long cooking, as in a slow cooker, will mellow the flavour of garlic.
- If you prefer, use ready-cooked prawns (thawed if frozen). You'll need about 75 g/3 oz. Add them about 5 minutes before the end of the cooking time so they can heat through.

mushroom and tuna pasta

1

¾-**1**hr
HIGH

A tomato and
cucumber salad

50 g/2 oz/¼ cup **Mascarpone cheese**

1 small **garlic clove**, crushed, or 2.5 ml/½ tsp **garlic purée** (paste)

A pinch of **dried mixed herbs**

200 ml/7 fl oz/scant 1 cup very hot (not boiling) **vegetable stock**

75 g/3 oz fresh or **frozen sliced mushrooms**

200 g/7 oz/small can of **tuna**, drained and flaked

50 g/2 oz dried **pasta shapes**

Salt and freshly ground black pepper

1 Put the Mascarpone, garlic and mixed herbs in the ceramic cooking pot. Gradually stir in the stock, a little at a time, until well blended.

2 Add the mushrooms, tuna and pasta, season with salt and pepper and stir gently until thoroughly mixed. Cover with the lid and switch on the slow cooker to Auto or High.

3 Cook for ¾–1 hour or until the pasta is cooked and the sauce is thick and creamy. Serve with a tomato and cucumber salad.

Cook's tips
- Mascarpone is an Italian soft cream cheese with a silky smooth texture and a light creamy taste. Ordinary full-fat cream cheese may be used instead, if preferred, but don't use a low-fat version as it will separate during cooking.
- A small can of salmon may be substituted for the tuna or, for a vegetarian version, omit the fish and stir in 15 ml/1 tbsp each of thawed frozen peas, sweetcorn and mixed sliced (bell) peppers.

beef, lamb & pork

The slow cooker is renowned for producing wonderful meat casseroles, stews and braises. Here it truly excels, making even the toughest cuts meltingly tender and developing and enhancing their flavour.

Beef, lamb and pork provide an excellent concentrated source of protein and many valuable nutrients, particularly the minerals iron and zinc. As a bonus, because there is no pre-frying of meat or onions in the recipes, most are healthily lower in fat.

In this chapter you'll find a variety of recipes to suit every taste and budget using braising steak, chops and minced (ground) meats to sausages, bacon and venison. There are classic winter warmers such as Braised Lamb with Cannellini (see pages 114–15), Sausage Supper (see pages 146–7) and Simple Irish Stew (see pages 110–11), but you'll also find plenty of lighter, more contemporary dishes such as Thai-spiced Pork with Veg (see pages 136–7) and Lamb with Aubergines (see pages 112–13).

beef, lamb & pork tips

- You can buy small amounts of minced beef from the butcher or at the supermarket meat counter (don't be embarrassed to ask). If you buy it in larger packs, divide it into smaller meal-sized portions and pack it into freezer bags. Flatten the meat slightly in the bags to make stacking easier and so that it thaws more quickly.

- Store meat in the coldest part of the fridge and, if raw, keep it away from cooked foods. Be guided by the 'use by' dates (or freeze in individual portions on the day of purchase); generally most diced meats, chops and steaks will keep in the fridge for 2–3 days.

- Always trim off excess fat before cooking.

- Most meat recipes can be frozen, so it is often worth making a larger quantity and freezing the rest for another day.

- Nearly all of these recipes make two servings to enable you to save time by either keeping half for the next day or freezing one portion for the future.

- Many require long, slow cooking, so you can prepare them in the morning and leave them all day to cook to perfection.

- Place the meat on top of vegetables in the slow cooker as it cooks more quickly.

- Use water, stock, wine, beer or fruit juice for cooking meat.

- Remember to try to use vegetables in season for the finest flavour.

new england braised beef

Chef's note

This traditional American one-pot meal contains succulent slow-simmered beef and baby vegetables. Many supermarkets now sell 'easy-carve mini beef roast' joints, but if you can't buy one, use a piece of lean chuck steak instead.

6 fresh or frozen **baby button onions**

450 ml/¾ pint/2 cups very hot (not boiling) **beef** or **vegetable stock**

10 ml/2 tsp **cider vinegar** or **white wine vinegar**

An **'easy-carve mini beef roast'**, approximately 225 g/8 oz

350 g/12 oz pack of **prepared mixed baby vegetables** (containing carrots, leeks, turnips etc.) or ½ × 750 g/1¾ lb **frozen vegetable 'stew pack'** (containing a mixture of whole baby and diced vegetables such as carrots, onions, swede (rutabaga) and turnips)

175 g/6 oz **baby new potatoes**, scrubbed

A large pinch of **dried thyme** or **mixed herbs**

Salt and freshly ground black pepper

¼ **Savoy cabbage**, cored and finely shredded, or 75 g/3 oz **frozen shredded cabbage**

1   If using fresh baby onions, put them in a bowl and pour over enough boiling water to cover. Leave until the water is tepid, then remove the onions and cut off the tops and root ends; the skins will slide off easily. Put the onions in the ceramic cooking pot and pour over enough of the stock to cover them. Add the vinegar. Cover with the lid and turn on the slow cooker to Low. Leave for a few minutes while measuring and preparing the remaining ingredients.

2   Place the beef on top of the onions, then surround with the fresh or frozen vegetables and the potatoes. Sprinkle the herbs over and season with salt and pepper. Pour over enough of the remaining stock to cover the ingredients.

3   Re-cover with the lid and cook for $3\frac{3}{4}$–$5\frac{3}{4}$ hours or until the beef and vegetables are just tender. (Check the onions by piercing with a sharp knife or skewer as these will take the longest to cook.)

4   Add the cabbage and increase the temperature to High. Cook for a further 15 minutes or until just tender. Carve the beef into thick slices and place half in a bowl or freezer container with half the vegetables and gravy and allow to cool. Serve the remainder straight away on a warm plate.

Second serving

• Either cover the cooled beef and chill in the fridge for the following day, or freeze for up to a month. If frozen, allow the beef to defrost in the fridge overnight. To serve, transfer to a saucepan and heat until piping hot.

Cook's tip

• Baby button onions are also used in Greek Stifado (see pages 98–9).

spiced beef with horseradish

2

4-6 hrs LOW

Creamed potatoes or rice and a green vegetable

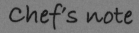
The warm spiciness of this casserole is achieved with a mixture of creamed horseradish, ginger and curry powder. It may sound an unusual combination but long, slow cooking develops and mellows all the flavours.

1 small **onion**, chopped, or 30 ml/2 tbsp **frozen diced onion**

15 ml/1 tbsp **creamed horseradish sauce**

10 ml/2 tsp **Worcestershire sauce**

250 ml/8 fl oz/1 cup very hot (not boiling) **beef stock**

5 ml/1 tsp **plain (all-purpose) flour**

2.5 ml/½ tsp medium **curry powder**

1.25 ml/¼ tsp **ground ginger**

2.5 ml/½ tsp **dark brown sugar**

350 g/12 oz cubed lean **braising** or **chuck steak**

Salt and freshly ground black pepper

30 ml/2 tbsp fresh or frozen chopped **parsley**

1   Put the onion in the ceramic cooking pot. Stir the horseradish and Worcestershire sauce into the stock and pour over the onion. Switch on the slow cooker to Low and leave for 3–4 minutes while measuring and preparing the rest of the ingredients.

2   Mix together the flour, curry powder, ginger and sugar in a bowl. Add the beef and toss to coat the cubes evenly in the spice mixture. Add to the pot and season with salt and pepper.

3   Cover with the lid and cook for 4–6 hours or until the beef is really tender.

4   Stir in the parsley, taste and re-season, if necessary. Spoon half the spiced beef into a bowl or freezer container and allow to cool. Serve the remainder at once with creamed potatoes or rice and a green vegetable.

Second serving

- Either cover the cooled spiced beef and chill in the fridge for the following day, or freeze for up to a month. If frozen, allow to defrost in the fridge overnight. To serve, heat gently in a saucepan, bubbling for a few minutes to ensure that the beef is piping hot.

Cook's tip

- Use ginger purée (paste) and curry paste instead of the ground ginger and curry powder, if you prefer.

crumble-topped beef casserole

2

3½-6 hrs
LOW

Green vegetables

Chef's note

Cooking in the slow cooker doesn't mean you can't enjoy meals with crunchy toppings such as this savoury crumble. It does take a little more effort as it's finished in the oven, but both the basic casserole and the crumble topping are easy to prepare.

For the beef casserole:

350 g/12 oz cubed lean **braising** or **chuck steak**

200 g/7 oz frozen **'root roasting' vegetables**

200 g/7 oz/small can of **tomatoes with herbs**

120 ml/4 fl oz/½ cup very hot (not boiling) **beef stock**

Salt and freshly ground black pepper

For the crumble topping:

50 g/2 oz/½ cup **plain (all-purpose) flour**

A pinch of **English mustard powder** (optional)

25 g/1 oz chilled **butter**, cut into small cubes

25 g/1 oz/¼ cup grated **Cheddar cheese**

1   Put the beef and vegetables in the ceramic cooking pot. Add the tomatoes and stock and season with salt and pepper. Cover with the lid and cook on Low for 3–5½ hours or until the beef and vegetables are very tender.

2   Meanwhile, to make the topping, put the flour, mustard powder and butter in a food processor and whiz together until the mixture resembles fine breadcrumbs. Add the cheese, season with salt and pepper and briefly process again to mix.

3   Just before the end of the casserole's cooking time, preheat the oven to 190°C/375°F/gas 5/fan oven 170°C. Spoon half of the casserole into an ovenproof dish, level the top, then sprinkle the crumble mixture over. Bake uncovered for 20–25 minutes until golden brown.

4   Spoon the remaining casserole into a bowl or freezer container and leave to cool.

5   Serve the crumble-topped casserole with some green vegetables.

Second serving

• Either cover the cooled casserole and chill in the fridge for the following day, or freeze for up to a month. If frozen, allow the casserole to defrost in the fridge overnight. To serve, heat gently in a saucepan with an extra 15 ml/1 tbsp of stock or water and allow to bubble for about 5 minutes.

Cook's tip

• Bags of frozen 'root roasting' vegetables usually contain a mixture of onions, carrots, parsnips and swede (rutabaga), all cut into small chunks.

mid-week pork meatloaf

2

3-5 hrs
HIGH

Creamed potatoes, a green vegetable and gravy

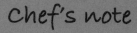
Chef's note

The slow cooker makes a great bain-marie (cooking in a dish over simmering water), as demonstrated by this tasty meatloaf. The addition of oats and grated carrots makes the meat go further, adds moistness and gives a great flavour.

30 ml/2 tbsp **milk**

2.5 ml/½ tsp **Dijon mustard**

15 g/½ oz/2 tbsp **porridge oats**

A little **butter** or **oil** for greasing

150 g/5 oz **lean minced (ground) beef**

150 g/5 oz **lean minced pork**

1 small **onion**, finely chopped, or 30 ml/2 tbsp **frozen diced onion**

1 **garlic clove**, crushed, or 5 ml/1 tsp **garlic purée** (paste)

1 **carrot**, coarsely grated, or 75 g/3 oz **ready-grated carrots**

2.5 ml/½ tsp **dried mixed thyme**

Salt and freshly ground black pepper

Opposite: Pork, Apple & Red Cabbage (see pages 130–31)

1 Blend together the milk and mustard in a mixing bowl, then sprinkle the oats over. Leave to soak for a few minutes.

2 Meanwhile, place an upturned saucer or metal pastry (paste) cutter in the base of the ceramic cooking pot and pour in about 2.5 cm/1 in of very hot (not boiling) water. Switch on the slow cooker to High.

3 Grease a 13–15 cm/5–6 in round fixed-base cake tin or soufflé dish and line the base with baking parchment.

4 Mix in the beef, pork, onion, garlic, carrot and thyme and season with salt and pepper. Transfer the mixture into the prepared tin or dish, levelling the top. Cover with lightly greased foil and place in the cooking pot on top of the saucer or pastry cutter. Pour in enough boiling water to come half-way up the side of the dish or tin.

5 Cover with the lid and cook for 3–5 hours or until the meatloaf is firm and a skewer inserted into the middle comes out hot. Carefully remove from the pot and leave to stand for 5 minutes before turning out and cutting into four wedges.

6 Place two wedges on a plate and leave to cool. Serve the remaining two wedges hot with creamed potatoes, a green vegetable and gravy.

Second serving

• Either cover the cooled meatloaf and chill in the fridge for the following day, or freeze for up to a month. If frozen, allow the beef to defrost in the fridge overnight. Reheat in a microwave or serve cold with a baked potato and a salad or coleslaw.

Opposite: Braised Lamb with Cannellini (see pages 114–115)

greek stifado

3-6 hrs **LOW**

Complete meal in itself

Chef's note

This Mediterranean casserole contains new potatoes, artichokes, broad beans and olives. Ideal for easy entertaining, it is simple to make – and comes out of the slow cooker smelling and tasting absolutely wonderful.

6 fresh or frozen **baby onions**

1 **garlic clove**, crushed, or 5 ml/1 tsp **garlic purée** (paste)

1.5 ml/¼ tsp **ground cumin**

1.5 ml/¼ tsp **ground cinnamon**

100 ml/3½ fl oz/scant ½ cup very hot (not boiling) **beef stock**

350 g/12 oz cubed lean **chuck** or **braising steak**

100 g/4 oz prepared mini **baby new potatoes**

100 g/4 oz **frozen broad (fava) beans**

25 g/1 oz stoned (pitted) **Kalamata olives**, roughly chopped

200 g/7 oz/small can of **chopped tomatoes with herbs**

100 ml/3½ fl oz/scant ½ cup full-bodied **red wine**

1 **bay leaf**

Salt and freshly ground black pepper

1   If using fresh baby onions, put them in a bowl and pour over enough boiling water to cover. Leave until the water is tepid, then remove the onions and cut off the tops and root ends; the skins will slide off easily.

2   Put the onions, garlic, cumin and cinnamon in the ceramic cooking pot and pour the stock over. Cover with the lid and switch on the slow cooker to Low. Leave for a few minutes while measuring and preparing the rest of the ingredients.

3   Add the beef, potatoes, beans and olives to the pot. Pour the tomatoes and wine over, add the bay leaf and season with salt and pepper. Re-cover with the lid and cook for 3–6 hours or until the onions and beef are tender.

4   Spoon half the casserole into a bowl or freezer container and allow to cool. Serve the rest straight away on a warm plate.

Second serving

• Either cover the cooled beef and chill in the fridge for the following day, or freeze for up to a month. If frozen, allow the beef to defrost in the fridge overnight. To serve, transfer to a saucepan and heat until piping hot.

Cook's tips

• Baby button onions are also used to make New England Braised Beef (see pages 90–91).

south american beef pot

1

4-6 hrs LOW

Complete meal in itself

Chef's note

A great way to jazz up minced beef, this hearty and satisfying one-pot meal contains chunks of potato and sliced peppers in a rich tomato sauce. It's finished with a creamy savoury egg sauce topping.

1 small **onion**, chopped, or 25 g/1 oz **frozen diced onion**

1 small **garlic clove**, crushed, or 2.5 ml/½ tsp **garlic purée** (paste)

100 ml/3½ fl oz/scant ½ cup very hot (not boiling) **beef stock**

100 g/4 oz **lean minced (ground) beef steak**

100 ml/3½ fl oz/scant ½ cup **passata** (sieved tomatoes)

1 small green (bell) **pepper**, halved, cored and sliced, or 150 g/5 oz **frozen sliced peppers**

100 g/4 oz **potato**, peeled and cut into 2 cm/¾ in dice

Salt and freshly ground black pepper

15 ml/1 tbsp fresh or frozen **chopped parsley**

1 **egg**

45 ml/3 tbsp **milk**

1   Put the onion in the cooking pot. Blend together the garlic and stock and pour over the onion. Switch on the slow cooker to Low and leave for a few minutes while measuring and preparing the rest of the ingredients.

2   Crumble the minced beef into the cooker with your fingers (this helps to stop it clumping together). Add the passata, pepper slices and potato, season with salt and pepper and stir well.

3   Cover with the lid and cook for $3\frac{1}{2}$–$5\frac{1}{2}$ hours or until the meat and vegetables are very tender.

4   Stir most of the parsley into the meat mixture. Beat together the egg, milk and a little salt and pepper until blended. Pour the egg mixture over the meat, re-cover with the lid and cook for a further 30 minutes or until the topping is set. Sprinkle with the remaining parsley before serving.

Cook's tip

• Passata is made from ripe tomatoes that have been puréed and sieved (strained) to remove the skin and seeds. It's sold in jars and cartons. Once opened, it will keep in the fridge for up to a week. Alternatively, decant it into small freezer containers and freeze for up to 2 months.

goulash with caraway seeds

2

4-6 hrs
LOW

Soured (dairy sour) cream or crème fraîche

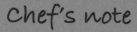

Chef's note

Conventional suet dumplings are almost impossible to make in the slow cooker as they need to be cooked in rapidly boiling stock for a fluffy texture. In this recipe, dumplings made from breadcrumbs and flavoured with herbs and caraway seeds are beautifully light.

1 small **onion**, finely chopped, or 25 g/1 oz **frozen diced onion**

1 small **garlic clove**, crushed, or 2.5 ml/½ tsp **garlic purée** (paste)

150 ml/¼ pint/⅔ cup very hot (not boiling) **beef stock**

350 g/12 oz cubed lean **chuck** or **braising steak**

5 ml/1 tsp **paprika**

¼ **white cabbage** or 75 g/3 oz frozen **shredded cabbage**

100 g/4 oz fresh or frozen **whole baby carrots**

200 g/7 oz/small can of **chopped tomatoes with herbs**

Salt and freshly ground black pepper

For the dumplings:

1 **egg**

15 ml/1 tbsp **milk**

15 ml/1 tbsp fresh or frozen **chopped parsley**

1.5 ml/¼ tsp **caraway seeds**

75 g/3 oz/1½ cups fresh **white breadcrumbs**

1   Put the onion and garlic in the ceramic cooking pot. Pour in the stock, cover with the lid and switch on the slow cooker to Low. Leave for a few minutes while measuring and preparing the remaining ingredients.

2   Sprinkle the beef cubes with the paprika. Finely shred the cabbage. Add the beef and cabbage to the pot with the carrots and tomatoes. Season with salt and pepper, then re-cover with the lid and cook for 4–6 hours or until the beef is very tender.

3   About 45 minutes before the end of the cooking time, turn up the slow cooker to High. To make the dumplings, beat together the egg and milk in a bowl. Stir in the parsley and caraway seeds and a little salt and pepper. Add the breadcrumbs and mix well. With wet hands, shape the dumpling mixture into eight walnut-sized balls. Add to the pot, re-cover with the lid and cook for a further 30 minutes.

4   Transfer half of the goulash and dumplings to a bowl and allow to cool. Serve the remainder at once, topped with a little soured cream or crème fraîche.

Second serving

• Cover the cooled goulash and dumplings and chill in the fridge for the following day. To serve, heat gently in a saucepan, bubbling for a few minutes, or microwave on High for 2–3 minutes.

frikadellers

2 **shallots**, finely sliced, or 30 ml/2 tbsp **frozen diced onion**

1 small **garlic clove**, crushed, or 2.5 ml/½ tsp **garlic purée** (paste)

1 **celery stick**, thinly sliced

½ red (bell) **pepper**, seeded and sliced, or 75 g/3 oz **frozen sliced peppers**

200 g/7 oz/small can of **chopped tomatoes**

100 ml/3½ fl oz/scant ½ cup boiling **beef stock**

Salt and freshly ground black pepper

For the meatballs:

1 slice of **white bread**

45 ml/3 tbsp **hot water**

100 g/4 oz **minced (ground) beef**

100 g/4 oz **minced pork**

A pinch of **ground allspice**

1   Put the shallots or diced onion, the garlic, celery and sliced pepper in the ceramic cooking pot. Pour the tomatoes and stock over and season with salt and pepper. Switch on the slow cooker to Low, cover with the lid and leave to cook for a few minutes while making the meatballs.

2   Tear the bread into small pieces and put in a bowl. Sprinkle the hot water over the bread, leave to soak for a minute or two, then mash with a fork until pulpy. Add the beef, pork and allspice and season with salt and pepper. Using your hands, mix all the ingredients together thoroughly.

3   With damp hands shape the mixture into 10 meatballs. Carefully drop the meatballs, one at a time, into the tomato sauce. Re-cover with the lid and cook for 2–3 hours or until the meatballs are cooked through and the vegetables in the sauce are tender.

4   Spoon half the meatballs and sauce into a bowl or freezer container and allow to cool. Serve the remaining meatballs and sauce with pasta.

Second serving

- Either cover the cooled meatballs and sauce and chill in the fridge for the following day, or freeze for up to a month. If frozen, allow the meatballs to defrost in the fridge overnight. To serve, transfer to a saucepan and heat until piping hot.

Cook's tip

- Always buy good-quality extra-lean mince. It may cost a little more, but is better value as it contains less fat.

savoury mince

2

4-7 hrs
LOW

Spaghetti

Chef's note

This basic mince mixture may be simply served as a Bolognese sauce, layered with sheets of pasta and ready-made white sauce to make a lasagne, or cooked with a large pinch of crushed dried chilli flakes and a can of kidney beans for a chilli con carne.

1 small **onion**, chopped, or 30 ml/2 tbsp **frozen diced onion**

1 small **garlic clove**, crushed, or 2.5 ml/½ tsp **garlic purée** (paste)

120 ml/4 fl oz/½ cup very hot (not boiling) **beef stock**

2 rashers (slices) of **lean back bacon**

1 **carrot**, diced, or 75 g/3 oz **frozen diced carrots**

1 **celery stick**, finely chopped

225 g/8 oz **lean minced (ground) beef** or **steak**

200 g/7 oz/small can of **chopped tomatoes**

60 ml/4 tbsp **red** or **white wine** or extra **stock**

5 ml/1 tsp **sun-dried tomato purée** (paste)

2.5 ml/½ tsp **dried mixed herbs**

Salt and freshly ground black pepper

1 Put the onion and garlic in the ceramic cooking pot and pour the stock over. Cover with the lid and switch on the slow cooker to Auto or Low. Leave for a few minutes while measuring and preparing the rest of the ingredients.

2 Cut the fat and rind off the bacon with kitchen scissors and snip the bacon into small pieces. Add to the pot with the carrot and celery. Crumble the minced beef into the cooker with your fingers (this helps to stop it clumping together). Add the tomatoes, wine or extra stock, the tomato purée and herbs.

3 Stir, then re-cover with the lid and cook on Auto for 4–5 hrs or on Low for 5–7 hours.

4 Stir with a fork to break up the meat, then season to taste with salt and pepper. Spoon half the savoury mince into a bowl or freezer container and allow to cool. Serve the remaining mince as a Bolognese sauce with spaghetti.

Second serving
• Either cover the cooled mince and chill in the fridge for the following day, or freeze for up to a month. If frozen, allow the mince to defrost in the fridge overnight. To serve, heat gently in a saucepan and allow to bubble for about 5 minutes until piping hot.

Cook's tip
• Other types of minced meat may be used as an alternative to beef, such as lamb, pork or turkey.

beef in red wine

2

6-8 hrs
HIGH

Mashed potatoes
and a green
vegetable

Chef's note

Cooking beef slowly, especially in wine, gives you a meltingly tender result. This simple version of the classic French dish is sure to become a favourite.

30 ml/2 tbsp **frozen diced onion**

50 g/2 oz rindless **smoked streaky bacon**, cut into small pieces

75 g/3 oz **baby button mushrooms**

350 g/12 oz **lean braising** or **chuck steak**, cut into 5 cm/ 2 in cubes

5 ml/1 tsp **plain (all-purpose) flour**

5 ml/1 tsp **garlic purée**

120 ml/4 fl oz/½ cup hot (not boiling) **beef stock**

100 ml/3½ fl oz/scant ½ cup **red wine**

A pinch of **dried thyme**

1 **bay leaf**

Salt and freshly ground black pepper

15 ml/1 tbsp chopped **fresh parsley**

1   Put the onion, bacon and mushrooms in the ceramic cooking pot and switch on the slow cooker to High,

2   Toss the meat in the flour, then add it to the pot.

3   Mix the garlic into the beef stock and wine and pour over the ingredients. Add the thyme and bay leaf and season with salt and pepper.

4   Cover with the lid, reduce the heat to Low and cook for 6–8 hours until the meat and vegetables are very tender.

5   Serve with mashed potatoes and a green vegetable.

Cook's tip

- You can buy miniature bottles or cans of red wine which are ideal for cooking. Always choose one which you also enjoy drinking as there will be some left over. A cheap wine will also ruin the flavour of any dish.

simple irish stew

Chef's note

Made in the traditional way without pre-browning the ingredients, this dish was originally prepared with a fatty cut of lamb and only potatoes and onions. In this up-to-date version, carrots and herbs are included for extra flavour and a lean lamb leg steak saves a lot of time.

1

5-7 hrs LOW

A vegetable such as peas or green beans (optional)

1 boneless **lean lamb leg steak**, about 150 g/5 oz

1 small **onion**, thinly sliced, or 30 ml/2 tbsp **frozen diced onion**

2.5 ml/½ tsp fresh or frozen **thyme leaves** or a pinch of **dried thyme**

Salt and freshly ground black pepper

225 g/8 oz **potatoes**, thinly sliced

1 **carrot**, sliced, or 75 g/3 oz **frozen sliced carrots**

1 **bay leaf**

150 ml/¼ pint/⅔ cup boiling **lamb, mild beef** or **vegetable stock**

1   Trim any excess fat from the lamb steak and cut into four pieces. Arrange the onion on the bottom of the ceramic cooking pot.

2   Seasoning between the layers with a little thyme and salt and pepper as you go, add a layer of potato slices, followed by a layer of carrots and the bay leaf, then finish with any remaining potatoes. Finally, top with the meat.

3   Pour the stock over the meat (if necessary, add a little more so that the meat is just covered). Cover with the lid and cook on Low for 5–7 hours or until the meat and vegetables are very tender.

4   Spoon the stew on to a warm plate or bowl. If liked, serve with an extra vegetable such as peas or green beans.

Cook's tips

• Although cooking the meat on top of the potatoes sounds unusual, it reflects the amount of time for each raw ingredient to cook. Meat takes less time than vegetables, so is placed furthest away from the heat source, which is under the base of the ceramic cooking pot.

• Other cuts of lamb may be used for this dish instead of the lamb leg steak, if preferred; try using trimmed boned shoulder of lamb cut into 2.5 cm/1 in chunks or 2 neck of lamb chops.

lamb with aubergines

2

5-7 hrs **LOW**

Pitta bread

Chef's note

This Greek-inspired dish contains chunks of tender lamb and aubergine in a rich tomato sauce flavoured with cumin. A spoonful of mint jelly gives the sauce a fresh herby flavour and adds just a hint of sweetness.

1 **red onion**, chopped, or 30 ml/2 tbsp **frozen diced onion**

1 **garlic clove**, crushed, or 2.5 ml/½ tsp **garlic purée** (paste)

A large pinch of **dried Mediterranean herbs** or **oregano**

5 ml/1 tsp **balsamic vinegar**

15 ml/1 tbsp **mint jelly**

100 ml/3½ fl oz/scant ½ cup very hot (not boiling) **lamb** or **vegetable stock**

1 small **aubergine** (eggplant), about 175 g/6 oz

5 ml/1 tsp **ground cumin**

225 g/8 oz ready-cubed **boneless lamb**

200 g/7 oz/small can of **chopped tomatoes**

Salt and freshly ground black pepper

Greek-style yoghurt

1 Put the onion, garlic and herbs in the ceramic cooking pot. Add the balsamic vinegar and mint jelly to the stock and stir until the jelly has dissolved. Pour over the onion mixture, cover with the lid and switch on the slow cooker to Low. Leave for a few minutes while measuring and preparing the rest of the ingredients.

2 Trim the ends off the aubergine and cut the flesh into cubes, about 2 cm/¾ in. Sprinkle the cumin over the lamb cubes and toss to lightly coat.

3 Add the aubergine, lamb and tomatoes to the pot and season with salt and pepper. Stir everything together, then cover with the lid and cook for 5–7 hours or until the lamb is really tender. Taste and re-season, if necessary.

4 Spoon half the lamb mixture into a bowl or freezer container and allow to cool. Serve the remainder at once, topped with a little Greek-style yoghurt. Pitta bread makes a good accompaniment.

Second serving

• Either cover the cooled lamb and chill in the fridge for the following day, or freeze for up to a month. If frozen, allow to defrost in the fridge overnight. To serve, heat gently in a saucepan, bubbling for a few minutes to ensure that the lamb is piping hot.

Cook's tip

• Don't be tempted to add more liquid to this dish at the start of cooking as the aubergine produces a lot of juices as it tenderises.

braised lamb with cannellini

 **1**

 **4-4½hrs LOW**

 New potatoes and a green vegetable

Chef's note

The perfect portion for one, lamb shanks are often sold individually or in pairs and become meltingly tender when slow cooked. Here, a dash of balsamic vinegar adds depth and a rich colour to the sauce. If you prefer to make two portions, simply double the ingredients.

1 small **onion**, chopped, or 25 g/1 oz **diced frozen onion**

1 small **garlic clove**, crushed, or 2.5 ml/½ tsp **garlic purée** (paste)

A large pinch of **dried Mediterranean herbs, thyme** or **oregano**

75 ml/3 fl oz/5 tbsp very hot (not boiling) **lamb** or **vegetable stock**

1 **lamb shank**

15 ml/1 tbsp **balsamic vinegar**

1 **carrot**, diced, or 75 g/3 oz **frozen sliced** or **diced carrots**

1 **celery stick**, thinly sliced (optional)

1 **bay leaf**

200 g/7 oz/small can of **chopped tomatoes**

Salt and freshly ground black pepper

½ × 400 g/14 oz/large can of **cannellini beans**

1   Put the onion, garlic and herbs in the ceramic cooking pot. Pour the stock over, cover with the lid and switch on the slow cooker to Low. Leave for 3–4 minutes while measuring and preparing the rest of the ingredients.

2   Put the lamb shank on top of the onion, then sprinkle the balsamic vinegar over the lamb. Add the carrot and celery, if using, filling in the gaps between the shank, and tuck in the bay leaf. Pour the tomatoes over the meat and vegetables and season with salt and pepper. If necessary, add a little more stock so that the lamb shank is just covered. Cover with the lid and cook for 3½–4 hours or until the lamb and vegetables are tender. Skim off any fat that has risen to the top.

3   Drain the beans in a sieve (strainer) and rinse with boiling water (this will shorten the time that they take to heat through). Add to the pot and cook on High for a further 15 minutes. Spoon on to a warm plate and serve at once with new potatoes and a green vegetable.

Cook's tips
- Use the remaining beans to make Chilli Bean Chowder (see pages 24–5) or Spiced Bean and Pumpkin Stew (see pages 206–7).
- If you are using a small slow cooker, make sure that you choose a short lamb shank that will fit in the ceramic cooking pot.
- Balsamic vinegar is rich, dark and mellow. Made in Modena in Northern Italy, it is fermented from grape juice for a minimum of 4 years and the most expensive versions for up to 40 years. It has a unique flavour, so don't use ordinary vinegar as a substitute in this dish.

lamb and sweet potato stew

 1

 **4-7** hrs LOW

 **Purple sprouting broccoli or curly kale**

1 small **onion**, finely chopped, or 30 ml/2 tbsp **frozen diced onion**

25 g/1 oz **pearl barley**

1 **lamb chop**, about 100 g/4 oz, trimmed of fat

1 **bay leaf**

A pinch of **dried thyme** or **dried mixed herbs**

150 g/5 oz **sweet potato**, peeled and cut into large chunks, or **frozen chunks of sweet potato**

250 ml/8 fl oz/1 cup boiling **lamb** or **vegetable stock**

Salt and freshly ground black pepper

1   Put the onion and barley in the ceramic cooking pot. Add the lamb chop and top with the bay leaf, then sprinkle with the herbs. Arrange the sweet potato chunks around the lamb.

2   Pour the stock over, adding a little more if necessary to just cover the potatoes, and season with salt and pepper. Switch on the slow cooker to Low, cover with the lid and cook for 4–6 hours or until the lamb and vegetables are tender.

3   Spoon the lamb and vegetables on to a warm serving plate, discarding the bay leaf. Serve with an extra vegetable such as purple sprouting broccoli or curly kale.

Second serving

- If you like, make double the quantity and serve the second portion the following day.

lamb with carrots and barley

 2

 **5-7** hrs LOW

 Potatoes and a green vegetable

Chef's note

It's worth making two portions and putting the second in the freezer for another day, but you can make half the amount if you prefer to make one serving. This is a tasty dish for winter days.

225 g/8 oz **braising lamb**, cubed

30 ml/2 tbsp **frozen diced onions**

2 **carrots**, thickly sliced

15 ml/1 tbsp **pearl barley**

A pinch of **dried thyme**

250 ml/8 fl oz/1 cup very hot (not boiling) **vegetable stock**

Salt and freshly ground black pepper

1   Place all the ingredients in the ceramic cooking pot, stir, and season with salt and pepper

2   Cover with the lid and cook on Low for 5–7 hours or until the meat and vegetables are very tender.

3   Spoon the stew on to a warm plate or bowl.

4   Serve with potatoes and a green vegetable.

Cook's tip
• Add a spoonful of tomato purée (paste) for extra flavour.

chinese braised lamb

1

2-4 hrs
LOW

Noodles or
prawn crackers

Chef's note

Here strips of lamb are cooked in an intensely flavoured sauce until beautifully tender. For a fast finish, serve with rice or 'instant' noodles, which are ready to serve after brief soaking in boiling stock or water.

5 ml/1 tsp **clear honey**

5 ml/1 tsp **dark soy sauce**

5 ml/1 tsp **smooth peanut butter**

10 ml/2 tsp **hoisin sauce**

A pinch of **Chinese five spice powder** or **ground cinnamon**

175 ml/6 fl oz/¾ cup very hot (not boiling) **vegetable stock**

150 g/5 oz **boneless lamb** such as leg or fillet

5 **spring onions** (scallions), trimmed and sliced

75 g/3 oz fresh or **frozen sliced mushrooms**

1   Put the honey, soy sauce, peanut butter, hoisin sauce and spice powder or cinnamon in the ceramic cooking pot. Add a little of the stock and stir until blended, then stir in the remaining stock.

2   Cut the lamb into strips about 2.5 cm × 1 cm/1 × ½ in. Add to the pot with the spring onions and mushrooms. Stir well, cover with the lid and cook for 2–4 hours on Low or until the lamb is very tender and the vegetables are cooked.

3   Serve with noodles or prawn crackers.

Variations
- Strips of turkey escalope, pork fillet or lean rump steak would make an excellent alternative to lamb.

Cook's tips
- Hoisin sauce is a thick and sticky brownish-red sauce made from soy beans, garlic, chilli, sugar and vinegar. It adds an authentic flavour to many Chinese-style dishes. Once opened, keep it in the fridge – it will last for several months.
- Dark soy sauce is richer and less salty than light, though you could use either for this dish. When a recipe contains soy sauce, always taste before seasoning as it is unlikely to need extra salt.

lamb and apricot tagine

 **2**

 **4-6 hrs LOW**

 Couscous

Chef's note

While this isn't an authentic Moroccan tagine recipe, it does contain all the essential flavourings, including cumin, cinnamon, lemon juice and a little harissa. It is named after the conical earthernware pot that cooks on gentle, even heat, allowing almost no moisture to escape. A slow cooker provides the perfect alternative.

1 small **onion**, chopped, or 30 ml/2 tbsp **frozen diced onion**

1 small **garlic clove**, crushed, or 2.5 ml/½ tsp **garlic purée** (paste)

A pinch of **dried thyme** or **dried mixed herbs**

2.5 ml/½ tsp **harissa paste**

15 ml/1 tbsp **sun-dried tomato purée** (paste)

350 ml/12 fl oz/1⅓ cups very hot (not boiling) **vegetable** or **lamb stock**

225 g/8 oz **boneless cubed lamb**

2.5 ml/½ tsp **ground cumin**

2.5 ml/½ tsp **ground turmeric**

2.5 ml/½ tsp **ground cinnamon**

50 g/2 oz/⅓ cup no-need-to-soak **dried apricots**, quartered

Salt and freshly ground black pepper

30 ml/2 tbsp fresh or frozen **chopped coriander** (cilantro)

15 g/½ oz/2 tbsp **toasted flaked (slivered) almonds** to garnish (optional)

1   Put the onion, garlic and herbs in the ceramic cooking pot. Blend together the harissa paste, tomato purée and stock and pour over the onion mixture. Cover with the lid and switch on the slow cooker to Low. Leave for 3–4 minutes while measuring and preparing the rest of the ingredients.

2   Put the lamb in a bowl and sprinkle the cumin, turmeric and cinnamon over. Mix together to coat the cubes evenly in the spice mixture. Add to the pot with the apricots and season with salt and pepper. Cover with the lid and cook for 4–6 hours or until the lamb is really tender.

3   Stir in the coriander and re-season, if necessary. Spoon half the tagine into a bowl or freezer container and allow to cool. Spoon the remainder on to a warm plate, sprinkle with the toasted almonds, if liked, and serve with couscous.

Second serving

• Either cover the cooled tagine and chill in the fridge for the following day, or freeze for up to a month. If frozen, allow to defrost in the fridge overnight. To serve, heat gently in a saucepan, bubbling for a few minutes to ensure that the lamb is piping hot.

lamb and lentil curry

 1

 4-5 hrs LOW

 Naan bread and popadoms

Chef's note

Red lentils soak up the cooking juices to make a thick spicy sauce in this curry. Cubes of beef or pork may be used instead of the lamb, if preferred. If you are short of time or inclination, use ready-made cucumber raita.

1 **onion**, chopped, or 40 g/1½ oz **frozen diced onion**

1 small **garlic clove**, crushed, or 2.5 ml/½ tsp **garlic purée** (paste)

5 ml/1 tsp grated **fresh root ginger** or **bottled ginger**

1.5 ml/¼ tsp **chilli paste** or a pinch of crushed dried **chilli flakes** or **chilli powder**

5 ml/1 tsp **korma** or other **mild curry paste**

150 ml/¼ pint/⅔ cup very hot (not boiling) **vegetable stock**

50 g/2 oz/⅓ cup **red lentils**

150 g/5 oz **boneless cubed lamb**

200 g/7 oz/small can of **chopped tomatoes**

Salt and freshly ground black pepper

For the cucumber raita:

5 cm/2 in piece of **cucumber**, finely chopped or grated

150 g/¼ pint/⅔ cup of **Greek-style** or **thick natural yoghurt**

5 ml/1 tsp chopped fresh **mint** or **coriander** (cilantro) or 2.5 ml/½ tsp of **bottled mint**, drained

1   Put the onion, garlic, ginger, chilli and curry paste in the ceramic cooking pot. Stir in a little of the stock and blend everything together, then pour in the remaining stock. Cover with the lid and switch on the slow cooker to Low. Leave for a few minutes while measuring and preparing the rest of the ingredients.

2   Rinse the lentils in a sieve (strainer) under cold running water, then add to the pot with the lamb and tomatoes. Cover and cook for 4–5 hours or until the lamb and lentils are very tender.

3   To make the cucumber raita, mix together the cucumber and yoghurt. Stir in the fresh mint or coriander and season with salt and pepper.

4   Taste and season the curry with salt and pepper. Serve straight away with warmed naan bread and popadoms.

Cook's tip

• If you enjoy spicy food, it's worth investing in a small jar of ready-chopped chillies; once opened they will keep in the fridge for 2–3 months. About 5 ml/1 tsp is the equivalent of one small chilli.

lamb with dill and vegetables

2

2-3hrs **LOW**

Green vegetable

Chef's note

This recipe has a real springtime feel, with its baby new potatoes, carrots and peas. The dill-flavoured sauce is thickened at the end of cooking but it only takes a moment.

225 g/8 oz **lean boneless lamb**, cubed

30 ml/2 tbsp chopped **fresh dill** (dill weed)

1 **bay leaf**

300 ml/½ pint/1¼ cups very hot (not boiling) **vegetable stock**

5 ml/1 tsp **lemon juice**

2 **onions**, chopped or 60 ml/ 4 tbsp **frozen diced onions**

100 g/4 oz **baby carrots**

200 g/7 oz **baby new potatoes**

Salt and white pepper

30 ml/2 tbsp **frozen peas**

2.5 ml/½ tsp **cornflour** (cornstarch)

30 ml/2 tbsp **single (light) cream**

1   Switch the slow cooker on to High.

2   Put the lamb, dill and bay leaf in the ceramic cooking pot and pour over the stock and lemon juice. Add the onion, carrots and potatoes and season to taste with salt and pepper.

3   Cover with the lid and cook on Low for 2–3 hours.

4   Turn the slow cooker up to High. Add the peas and discard the bay leaf.

5   Blend together the cornflour, cream and a little water, if necessary, to make a smooth liquid. Stir into the sauce and cook for a further 15 minutes until thickened and tender.

6   Serve with a green vegetable.

Second serving
• Try serving this with crusty bread.

lancashire hotpot

Good, honest food! The meat and vegetables of this tasty dish are never browned first and the dish relies on long slow cooking to bring out all the flavours. There is a little bit of preparation but it is well worth it.

2

4-6 hrs LOW

Mushy peas

4 middle neck or loin **lamb chops**

450 g/1 lb **potatoes**, thinly sliced

1 **onion**, sliced or 30 ml/2 tbsp **frozen diced onion**

1 **carrot**, sliced

1 **leek**, sliced

2.5 ml/½ tsp **dried mixed herbs**

250 m/8 fl oz/1 cups very hot (not boiling) **lamb** or **beef stock**

Salt and freshly ground black pepper

1   Switch the slow cooker to High.

2   Trim the lamb chops of excess fat. Place a layer of sliced potatoes in the base of the ceramic cooking pot and top with sliced onion, carrot and leek. Sprinkle with some dried herbs and season with salt and pepper.

3   Place four of the chops on top, then repeat the layers of potatoes, vegetables and seasoning and top with the remaining chops. Finish with a generous layer of potatoes.

4   Pour over the stock, then cover with the lid.

5   Either cook on High for 1 hour then reduce the heat to Low for a further 2–3 hours until tender, or cook on Low for 4–6 hours.

6   Serve with mushy peas.

Cook's tip

- Although not included in a 'classic' Lancashire hotpot, you could add other vegetables as well, such as a handful of thickly sliced button mushrooms or a stick of celery.

pork with apple and red cabbage

1

3-5 hrs LOW

Creamed potatoes

Red cabbage slowly cooked with crisp, tart apples, such as a Granny Smith, and a dash of vinegar is a delicious foil for pork. Some creamy mashed potato – bought ready-made if you prefer – is all that's needed to complete the meal.

1 small red or white **onion**, chopped, or 30 ml/2 tbsp **frozen diced onion**

150 ml/¼ pint/⅔ cup very hot (not boiling) **chicken** or **vegetable stock**

150 g/5 oz **cubed pork** such as shoulder or tenderloin

1.5 ml/¼ tsp **caraway seeds**

175 g/6 oz **red cabbage**, finely shredded

1 small eating (dessert) **apple**, peeled, cored and thinly sliced

15 ml/1 tbsp **raisins** (optional)

Salt and freshly ground black pepper

5 ml/1 tsp **light brown sugar**

5 ml/1 tsp **red wine vinegar**

1 Put the onion in the ceramic cooking pot. Pour about half of the stock over, cover with the lid and switch on the slow cooker to Low. Leave for a few minutes while measuring and preparing the remaining ingredients.

2 Sprinkle the pork with the caraway seeds. Put the cabbage, apple slices and raisins, if using, on top of the onion, layering them up and seasoning with a little salt and pepper as you go. Put the pork on top. Mix together the sugar, vinegar and remaining stock and pour over the pork.

3 Cover with the lid and cook for 3–5 hours or until the pork and cabbage are very tender. Transfer to a warm plate and serve at once with creamed potatoes.

Cook's tip
• Ginger makes a good alternative flavouring to caraway seeds. Use 5 ml/1 tsp of grated fresh root ginger or bottled ginger and stir in with the sugar and vinegar.

spicy pork and apricots

2

3-5 hrs **LOW**

Rice and a green vegetable

Chef's note

Apricots have a natural affinity with pork and add a sweetness to the sauce. Some plain boiled or steamed rice and a fresh green vegetable is all that is needed to complete the meal.

1 small **onion**, chopped, or 30 ml/2 tbsp **frozen diced onion**

1 **garlic clove**, crushed, or 5 ml/1 tsp **garlic purée** (paste)

1.5 ml/¼ tsp crushed dried **chilli flakes** or a pinch of **chilli powder**

2.5 ml/½ tsp grated **fresh root ginger** or **bottled ginger**

2.5 ml/½ tsp **cumin seeds** (optional)

100 ml/3½ fl oz/scant ½ cup very hot (not boiling) **vegetable stock**

225 g/8 oz **pork tenderloin** or **fillet**

75 g/3 oz/½ cup ready-to-eat **dried apricots**

100 ml/3½ fl oz/scant ½ cup **passata** (sieved tomatoes)

Salt and freshly ground black pepper

15 ml/1 tbsp fresh or frozen **chopped coriander** (cilantro)

1   Put the onion, garlic, chilli, ginger and cumin seeds, if using, in the ceramic cooking pot. Pour in the stock, cover with the lid and switch on the slow cooker to Low. Leave for a few minutes while measuring and preparing the rest of the ingredients.

2   Thinly slice the pork and snip the apricots into quarters using kitchen scissors. Add to the pot with the passata, then season with salt and pepper. Re-cover and cook for 3–5 hours or until the onions are tender and the pork is cooked. Stir in the coriander.

3   Spoon half the spicy pork and apricot mixture into a bowl or freezer container and leave to cool. Spoon the rest on to a warm serving plate and serve straight away with boiled or steamed rice and a green vegetable.

Second serving

- Either cover the cooled mixture in the fridge for the following day, or freeze for up to a month. If frozen, allow to defrost in the fridge overnight. To serve, heat gently in a saucepan with an extra tablespoonful of stock or water and allow to bubble for about 5 minutes to ensure that the pork is piping hot.

pork chops in barbecue sauce

2

4-6 hrs
LOW

Rice and a green vegetable or a jacket potato and coleslaw

Chef's note

Pork lends itself to sweet and sour type sauces as they offset the richness of the meat. Serve with plain or stir-fried rice and a green vegetable such as broccoli or mangetout (snow peas) or a jacket potato and bought coleslaw.

2 boneless **pork loin chops**, about 150 g/5 oz each

45 ml/3 tbsp **orange juice**

15 ml/1 tbsp **clear honey**

15 ml/1 tbsp **dry sherry**

15 ml/1 tbsp **dark soy sauce**

5 ml/1 tsp **Dijon mustard**

15 ml/1 tbsp **tomato purée** (paste)

Freshly ground black pepper

1   Trim all the fat off the chops and place them in the ceramic cooking pot.

2   In a small bowl, blend together the orange juice, honey, sherry, soy sauce, mustard, tomato purée and a little black pepper.

3   Pour the sauce mixture over the chops and turn on the slow cooker to Low. Cover with the lid and top with a folded tea towel (dish cloth).

4   Cook for 4–6 hours or until the pork is very tender. Transfer one of the chops to a bowl or freezer container and allow to cool. Stir the sauce, then spoon half over the chop.

5   Serve the other chop and the rest of the sauce on a warm plate, accompanied with rice and a green vegetable or a jacket potato and coleslaw.

Second serving
• Either cover the cooled mixture and chill in the fridge for the following day, or freeze for up to a month. If frozen, allow to defrost in the fridge overnight. To serve, transfer to a saucepan and heat until piping hot.

Cook's tips
• If you haven't any sherry, substitute it with dry white wine, extra orange juice or water.
• You probably won't need to season the sauce with salt as there is plenty in the soy sauce already.
• Covering the slow cooker lid with a folded tea towel will stop steam evaporating and prevent the dish drying out.

thai-spiced pork with veg

2

4-5 hrs
LOW

Rice and
steamed pak
choi or baby

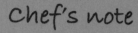

Chef's note

This has all the flavour of
a stir-fry without the
hassle of last-minute
cooking. Using lean pork
fillet and cooking on Auto
or Low ensures that the
meat will be tender while
the vegetables retain
their shape and texture.

225 g/8 oz **pork fillet**

8 **spring onions** (scallions)

1 small red (bell) **pepper** or 150
g/ 5 oz **frozen mixed sliced
peppers**

200 g/7 oz pack of **mixed baby
vegetables** such as carrots, mini
sweetcorn and mangetout (snow
peas)

15 ml/1 tbsp **Thai red curry
paste**

15 ml/1 tbsp **nam pla fish sauce**
or **light soy sauce**

400 ml/14 oz/large can of
coconut milk

30 ml/2 tbsp fresh or frozen
chopped coriander (cilantro)

1 Cut the pork fillet into 1 cm/½ in slices. Trim the spring onions, then slice diagonally into 2 cm/¾ in lengths. If using a fresh pepper, cut in half and remove all the white pith and seeds, then cut into thin slices. Trim the baby vegetables as necessary.

2 Layer up the pork and prepared vegetables in the ceramic cooking pot. Blend together the Thai red curry paste, nam pla fish sauce or soy sauce and a little of the coconut milk in a jug, then stir in the rest of the coconut milk. Pour over the pork and vegetables.

3 Cover with the lid and cook on Auto for 3 hours or on Low for 4–5 hours or until the pork and baby vegetables are tender. Stir in the coriander.

4 Spoon half the spiced pork mixture into a bowl and allow to cool. Serve the remainder at once with boiled or steamed rice and steamed pak choi or baby spinach.

Second serving

• Cover the cooled spiced pork and chill in the fridge for the following day. To serve, heat gently in a saucepan, bubbling for a few minutes to ensure that the pork is piping hot. This dish is not suitable for freezing.

Cook's tip

• Nam pla is a thin brown fish sauce that's an essential ingredient of Thai food. It has a salty taste and fishy aroma, but long-cooking – as here – reduces this to add a richness and depth of flavour.

mexican pork tacos

2

4 hrs HIGH

Corn tortillas, soured (dairy sour) cream and guacamole

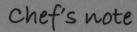

Chef's note

It's worth making a larger quantity of this tasty dish and enjoying it on more than one occasion!

30 ml/2 tbsp **frozen diced onion**

1 **pork tenderloin**

1 red (bell) **pepper**, seeded and diced

A pinch of **chilli flakes**

200 g/7 oz/1 small can **chopped tomatoes**

2.5 ml/½ tsp **ground cumin**

½ tsp **garlic purée**

½ tsp **dried oregano**

A pinch of **cayenne**

1 **green chilli**, diced

½ × 200 g/7 oz/1 small can **sweetcorn (corn)**

15 ml/1 tbsp **tomato purée (paste)**

1   Place all the ingredients in the slow cooker and stir well. Cover and cook on High for 4 hours until the meat is really tender.

2   Remove the pork to a chopping board and keep it warm.

3   If the sauce has not thickened to your liking, cook for another 30 minutes until further reduced.

4   Shred the pork using two forks to pull the meat apart. Stir the meat back into the sauce.

5   To serve, wrap the pork mixture in warmed corn tortillas and serve with soured cream and guacamole.

Second serving

- Cool the pork mixture, then chill in the fridge. Either serve the next day or freeze and use within three months.

spicy maple ribs

1

4-5 hrs **HIGH**

Salad and crusty rolls

Chef's note

These are the ultimate finger food. Made wonderfully tender in the slow cooker, the ribs are coated in a rich toffee-coloured sauce, so make sure you have plenty of paper napkins and a finger bowl ready before you start eating.

225 g/8 oz **pork spare ribs**

15 ml/1 tsp **garlic purée**

15 ml/1 tbsp **tomato ketchup** (catsup)

15 ml/1 tbsp **maple syrup**

5 ml/1 tsp **soft dark brown sugar**

5 ml/1 tsp **Dijon mustard**

10 ml/2 tsp **white** or **red wine vinegar**

15 ml/1 tbsp **Worcestershire sauce**

30 ml/2 tbsp **orange** or **apple juice**

1   Trim any excess fat from the ribs, then put them in the ceramic cooking pot in a single layer, if possible. Switch on the slow cooker to High or Auto.

2   Stir together all the remaining ingredients, then pour the sauce over the ribs, turning them to coat.

3   Cover with the lid and cook for 1 hour, then leave on Auto or reduce the temperature to Low and continue to cook for a further 3–4 hours.

Cook's tips

- If you prefer a very thick sauce, pour the sauce into a pan and let it bubble over a medium-high heat until reduced by half.
- Maple-flavoured syrup isn't suitable for these sticky ribs; do use pure maple syrup.

chilli with chorizo

2 hrs LOW

Guacamole, soured (dairy sour) cream and crusty bread

100 g/4 oz **chorizo**, cut into chunks

1 small **onion**, chopped or 30 ml/2 tbsp **frozen diced onion**

400 g/14 oz/1 large can **chopped tomatoes**

½ x 400 g/14 oz/large can **black-eyed or pinto beans**, rinsed and drained

Salt and freshly ground black pepper

1   Put all the ingredients into the slow cooker and mix well.

2   Cover with the lid and cook on Low for about 2 hours until rich and thick.

3   Serve with guacamole, soured cream and crusty bread to mop up the sauce.

Cook's tips

- This sauce also works well with meatballs.
- Black-eyed beans are also used in Caribbean-style Chicken (see pages 180–1)

ham hock and lentil braise

2

6-8 hrs **LOW**

Country-style crusty bread

Chef's note

This rustic stew makes the perfect supper dish. A ham hock braised until the meat is almost falling from the bone creates a delicious stock for the lentil and vegetable mixture. Serve with some crusty bread to complete the meal.

1 **ham hock**, about 1.25 kg/2½ lb

1 small **onion**, chopped, or 30 ml/2 tbsp **frozen diced onion**

About 400 ml/14 fl oz/1¾ cups very hot (not boiling) **vegetable stock**

150 g/5 oz **Puy lentils**

1 **carrot**, diced, or 75 g/3 oz **frozen diced carrots**

1 **bay leaf**

30 ml/2 tbsp fresh or frozen **chopped parsley**

Freshly ground black pepper

1 Put the ham hock in a large heatproof bowl or saucepan and pour over enough boiling water to cover. Leave for 3–4 minutes, then carefully drain off the water and briefly rinse the hock under cold running water.

2 Meanwhile, put the onion in the ceramic cooking pot. Pour over about half of the stock, cover with the lid and switch on the slow cooker to Low. Rinse the lentils in a sieve (strainer) under cold running water. Put the ham hock on top of the onion, then spoon the lentils and carrot around it. Tuck in the bay leaf, then pour in enough of the remaining stock to just cover the ham hock.

3 Re-cover with the lid and cook for 6–8 hours or until the meat and lentils are very tender. Carefully remove the ham hock. Re-cover the slow cooker and turn up the heat to High. Strip off the skin and fat from the ham with a knife. Remove the meat from the bone and shred it into small pieces.

4 Skim any fat off the top of the lentil mixture and remove the bay leaf. Return the pieces of ham to the slow cooker and stir in the parsley and a little freshly ground black pepper. Transfer half of the ham and lentil mixture to a bowl or freezer container and allow to cool.

5 Heat the remainder in the slow cooker for about 15 minutes until piping hot or quickly reheat in a saucepan on the hob. Serve in a warm bowl with country-style crusty bread.

Cook's tip
• Most butchers and supermarkets sell ham hocks (cured knuckles of pork). They vary in size, so choose one that is about 1.25 kg/2½ lb, which will provide two generous servings.

sausage supper

 1

 **3-5** hrs LOW

 Baked beans

Chef's note

Sausages should be precooked before adding to the slow cooker or the resulting dish will be greasy and the sausages themselves pale and uninviting. Ready-cooked mini sausages are used in this tasty all-in-one hotpot. If you're really hungry, serve with baked beans.

1 small **onion**, chopped, or 30 ml/2 tbsp **frozen diced onion**

10 ml/2 tsp **sun-dried tomato purée** (paste)

2.5 ml/½ tsp **dried mixed herbs**

A dash of **Worcestershire sauce** (optional)

150 ml/¼ pint/⅔ cup hot (not boiling) **beef** or **vegetable stock**

Salt and freshly ground black pepper

150 g/5 oz **mini new potatoes**, quartered

1 **carrot**, thinly sliced, or 75 g/ 3 oz **frozen sliced carrots**

8 **cooked mini sausages**

1   Put the onion, tomato purée, herbs and Worcestershire sauce, if using, in the ceramic cooking pot. Stir in a little of the stock and blend everything together, then stir in about half of the remaining stock. Cover with the lid and switch on the slow cooker to Low. Leave for 3–4 minutes while measuring and preparing the rest of the ingredients.

2   Seasoning between the layers with salt and pepper as you go, scatter the potato quarters over the onion mixture, followed by the carrot slices and finally top with the sausages.

3   Pour the remaining stock over the sausages (if necessary, add a little more so that they are just covered). Cover with the lid and cook for 3–5 hours or until the vegetables are very tender. Serve on a warm plate.

Cook's tips

- Instead of Worcestershire sauce, stir 2.5 ml/½ tsp of Dijon or wholegrain mustard into the stock.
- Sun-dried tomato purée contains lots of additional seasonings including chillies, garlic, oregano and capers, so it gives extra flavour without the need for lots of individual ingredients.
- Instead of bought mini sausages, you could use two or three leftover cooked sausages instead. Cut each in half.

barley, bacon and sausages

1

1¾-2 hrs
LOW

Complete meal in itself

Chef's note

Barley is a much underrated grain and rarely used, except as a thickener for casseroles. This is a great pity as it has a satisfying texture and makes a great alternative to rice. Here, its slightly nutty taste works brilliantly with bacon and sausages.

5 ml/1 tsp **sun-dried tomato purée** (paste)

250 ml/8 fl oz/1 cup very hot (not boiling) **vegetable stock**

3 **spring onions** (scallions), trimmed and sliced

1 **celery stick**, thinly sliced

1 rasher (slice) of **smoked back bacon**

75 g/3 oz/scant ½ cup **pearl barley**

6 **cooked mini sausages**

Salt and freshly ground black pepper

75 g/3 oz/3 tbsp **frozen peas**

1 Put the tomato purée in the ceramic cooking pot and pour in a spoonful or two of the stock. Stir until blended, add the spring onions and celery, then pour in the rest of the stock. Switch on the slow cooker to Low and leave for a few minutes while measuring and preparing the rest of the ingredients.

2 Remove the rind and fat from the bacon, then snip the bacon into small pieces with kitchen scissors. Add the barley, bacon and sausages to the pot and season with salt and pepper. Cover and cook for $1\frac{1}{2}$–$1\frac{3}{4}$ hours or until the barley is tender.

3 While the barley is cooking, spread out the peas on a piece of kitchen paper (paper towel) on a plate to allow them to defrost. Stir them into the pilaf, then cover and cook for a final 10 minutes to heat through the peas. Spoon the pilaf on to a warm plate and serve straight away.

Cook's tips
- Other frozen vegetables such as sweetcorn or mixed vegetables may be used instead of the peas.
- Pearl barley is husked and steamed and has a mild, sweet flavour and chewy texture. It is more easily available than pot barley, which is the whole grain with just the inedible outer husk removed. Either can be used in this recipe, but if using pot barley allow extra cooking time and a little more stock.

sausage and potato pot

1

4 hrs **LOW**

Wholemeal toast or crusty bread rolls

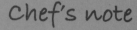

Chef's note

This is a simple and tasty dish, easily put together in the morning to be ready when you come home from work.

200 g/7 oz/1 small can of **tomatoes**

15 ml/1 tbsp **breadcrumbs**

2.5 ml/½ tsp **garlic purée**

A pinch of **paprika**

A pinch of **chilli flakes**

3–4 pre-cooked **turkey sausages**

1 **potato**, cut into chunks

15 ml/1 tbsp **frozen diced onion**

½ **courgette** (zucchini), sliced

30 ml/2 tbsp grated **Cheddar cheese**

1   Put the tomatoes and their juice in the slow cooker and stir in the onion and seasonings.

2   Push the sausages, potatoes and courgette under the sauce. Cover and cook on Low heat for 4 hours.

3   Remove the sausages and slice them thickly, then stir them back into the sauce with the breadcrumbs.

4   Serve sprinkled with the cheese.

Cook's tip

• You can use any kind of sausage for this dish.

venison with cranberries

2

4-6 hrs
LOW

Mashed potato
and a green
vegetable

Chef's note

Full of flavour, yet low in
saturated fat, venison
makes a healthy
alternative to beef for a
casserole. Make sure you
use venison shoulder or
haunch for this dish,
rather than an expensive
prime cut; the long-slow
cooking will tenderise
the meat and bring out
its flavour.

225 g/8 oz **boneless casserole
venison**

150 ml/¼ pint/⅔ cup **red wine**

30 ml/2 tbsp **cranberry sauce**

1 **garlic clove**, crushed, or
5 ml/1 tsp **garlic purée** (paste)

2.5 ml/½ tsp **dried thyme** or
mixed herbs

1 small **onion**, chopped, or
30 ml/2 tbsp **frozen diced onion**

150 ml/¼ pint/⅔ cup very hot (not
boiling) **beef stock**

1 rasher (slice) of **back bacon**

2 **carrots**, halved lengthways and
cut into 2.5 cm/1 in chunks, or
175 g/6 oz **frozen baby carrots**

**Salt and freshly ground black
pepper**

1   Cut the venison into 4 cm/1½ in cubes. Place in a bowl and pour the wine over. Add the cranberry sauce, garlic and herbs and leave to marinate for a few minutes while measuring and preparing the rest of the ingredients.

2   Put the onion in the ceramic cooking pot. Pour in the stock, cover with the lid and switch on the slow cooker to Low.

3   Cut the rind and fat off the bacon, then snip the bacon into small pieces with kitchen scissors. Add to the pot with the venison and marinade and the carrots. Season with salt and pepper.

4   Cover and cook for 4–6 hours or until the meat is very tender and the vegetables are cooked. Spoon half the casserole into a bowl or freezer container and allow to cool. Serve the remainder at once with creamy mashed potato and a green vegetable.

Second serving

• Either cover the cooled casserole and chill in the fridge for the following day, or freeze for up to a month. If frozen, allow to defrost in the fridge overnight. To serve, heat gently in a saucepan, bubbling for a few minutes to ensure that the venison is piping hot.

Cook's tips

• Beef stewing steak may be used instead of venison, if you prefer, and redcurrant jelly (clear conserve) rather than cranberry sauce.
• Let the venison marinate at room temperature for 30 minutes before cooking if you have time (or for up to 12 hours in the fridge, if you prefer). This not only allows the flavour to penetrate the meat but also helps to tenderise it.

chicken, turkey & duck

For succulence, flavour and versatility, chicken and poultry is hard to beat and there are many cuts to choose from to suit solo servings, including breasts, quarters, thighs and mini chicken fillets.

From casseroles to curries, there are recipes in this chapter to suit every taste and season – classics such as Coq au Vin (see pages 170–1), Normandy Chicken (see pages 160–1) and Duck with Orange Sauce (see pages 190–1) and more adventurous dishes including Hot and Spicy Mexican Chicken (see pages 168–9) and Poussin with Pear Stuffing (see pages 176–7).

Lean and healthy, chicken is full of protein and B vitamins and, if you're trying to reduce your red meat intake, minced chicken and turkey make an excellent alternative to minced beef, lamb or pork in most dishes.

chicken, turkey & duck tips

- Generally, chicken portions and breasts are less expensive if bought in larger packs, so straight after purchase split them into individual servings, wrap them well and freeze any that you won't be using within a day or two. They will keep for up to 3 months in the freezer.

- Defrost overnight in the fridge and always check that chicken is thoroughly thawed before adding to the slow cooker.

- You should also make sure that larger pieces such as quarters and thighs are thoroughly cooked before serving by piercing at the thickest point; the juices should run clear and not be at all pink, or test with a meat thermometer.

one-pot chicken casserole

2

3-5 hrs LOW

Complete meal in itself

Chef's note

This Italian-style chicken casserole is a whole meal in itself, so there's no need to cook extra vegetables to accompany it. Chunks of chicken breast and potatoes are slow cooked in a stock flavoured with sun-dried tomato and olives, so they soak up all the lovely flavour as they gently simmer.

1 small **onion**, chopped, or 30 ml/2 tbsp **frozen diced onion**

2.5 ml/½ tsp **dried Mediterranean** or **mixed herbs**

1 **garlic clove**, crushed, or 2.5 ml/½ tsp **garlic purée** (paste)

15 ml/1 tbsp **sun-dried tomato purée** (paste)

250 ml/8 fl oz/1 cup very hot (not boiling) **chicken stock**

225 g/8 oz **potatoes**, peeled

2 skinless, boneless **chicken breasts**

1 small red or yellow (bell) **pepper**, seeded and sliced, or 150 g/5 oz **frozen sliced peppers**

6 stoned (pitted) **black olives**

200 g/7 oz/small can of **chopped tomatoes**

Freshly ground black pepper

1   Put the onion, herbs, garlic and tomato purée in the ceramic cooking pot. Stir in a little of the stock and blend everything together, then stir in about half of the remaining stock. Cover with the lid and switch on the slow cooker to Auto or Low. Leave for a few minutes while measuring and preparing the rest of the ingredients.

2   Cut the potatoes into chunks about 2.5 cm/1 in. Trim the chicken breasts, if necessary, and cut each one into three pieces. Add the potatoes to the pot, top with the sliced peppers and olives, then place the pieces of chicken on top.

3   Stir the chopped tomatoes into the remaining chicken stock and season with black pepper. Pour over the chicken. Cover with the lid and cook for 3–5 hours or until the chicken and vegetables are tender and cooked through.

4   Taste the sauce and re-season, if necessary. Spoon half the casserole into a bowl or freezer container and allow to cool. Serve the remainder at once on a warm plate.

Second serving

- Either cover the cooled casserole and chill in the fridge for the following day, or freeze for up to a month. If frozen, allow to defrost in the fridge overnight. To serve, heat gently in a saucepan, bubbling for a few minutes to ensure that the chicken is piping hot.

Cook's tip

- The olives will add a salty flavour to the casserole, so taste at the end of cooking and season with a little salt, if desired.

ginger chicken and pineapple

2

3-5 hrs LOW

Rice and a green vegetable

Chef's note

Tender chicken with a taste of the tropics; it's well worth keeping a can of pineapple pieces in the kitchen cupboard. Make sure you choose pineapple in juice – rather than in syrup – for this delicious dish.

1 small **onion**, chopped, or 30 ml/2 tbsp **frozen diced onion**

1 **garlic clove**, crushed, or 2.5 ml/½ tsp **garlic purée** (paste)

2 cm/¾ in piece of **fresh root ginger**, peeled and finely chopped, or 5 ml/1 tsp **bottled ginger**

100 ml/3½ fl oz/scant ½ cup very hot (not boiling) **chicken stock**

4 skinless **chicken thighs**

Salt and freshly ground black pepper

200 g/7 oz/small can of **pineapple pieces in juice**

1   Put the onion, garlic and ginger in the ceramic cooking pot. Pour the stock over and switch on the slow cooker to Auto.

2   Season the chicken thighs with salt and pepper and place them on top of the onion mixture. Tip the pineapple pieces and all the juice over the chicken.

3   Cover with the lid and cook for 3–5 hours or on Low for 4–5 hours or until the chicken is cooked through and tender.

4   Spoon two chicken thighs and half the pineapple mixture into a bowl or freezer container and allow to cool. Serve the remainder at once with boiled or steamed rice and a green vegetable such as broccoli or mangetout (snow peas).

Second serving

• Either cover the cooled chicken and chill in the fridge for the following day, or freeze for up to a month. If frozen, allow to defrost in the fridge overnight. To serve, heat gently in a saucepan, bubbling for a few minutes to ensure that the chicken is piping hot.

Cook's tip

• Chicken thighs still on the bone are preferable for this dish as the chicken will be more flavoursome. If you use boneless chicken thighs, reduce the cooking time by up to 1 hour.

normandy chicken

2

3-5 hrs
LOW

French bread or creamed potatoes and green beans

1 small **onion**, chopped, or 30 ml/2 tbsp **frozen diced onion**

1 **garlic clove**, crushed, or 5 ml/1 tsp **garlic purée** (paste)

4 skinless **chicken thighs**

1 **celery stick**, sliced (optional)

Salt and freshly ground black pepper

1 **red apple**, cored and sliced into wedges

150 ml/¼ pint/⅔ cup **dry cider**

150 ml/¼ pint/⅔ cup boiling **chicken stock**

30 ml/2 tbsp fresh or frozen **chopped parsley**

30 ml/2 tbsp **crème fraîche**

Opposite: Normandy Chicken (see above)

1 Put the onion and garlic in the ceramic cooking pot. Arrange the chicken thighs on top, then pack the celery, if using, around the sides of the chicken. Season with salt and pepper.

2 Place the apple wedges on top of the chicken, then pour the cider and stock over. Cover with the lid and switch on the slow cooker to Auto.

3 Cook for 3–5 hours or until the chicken and vegetables are tender. Stir in the parsley, then transfer two of the chicken thighs and half the apples and gravy to a bowl or freezer container and cool.

4 Stir half the crème fraîche into the remaining casserole juices and serve on a warm plate. Serve with crusty French bread or creamed potatoes and steamed green beans.

Second serving

- Either cover the cooled mixture and chill in the fridge for the following day, or freeze for up to a month. If frozen, allow to defrost in the fridge overnight. To serve, transfer to a saucepan and heat until piping hot, stirring in the crème fraîche just before serving.

Cook's tip

- Two skinned chicken supremes (chicken breasts still on the bone) may be used instead of the thighs.
- For extra flavour, blend 2.5 ml/½ tsp of Dijon mustard with the crème fraîche before adding.
- Another recipe that includes crème fraîche is Macaroni Cheese (see pages 44–5).

Opposite: Chicken in Red Pepper Sauce (see pages 162–3)

chicken in red pepper sauce

2

3-5hrs
LOW

Tagliatelle or
rice

Chef's note

Here chicken and a red
pepper are gently
braised in stock and
white wine or orange
juice. The cooking juices
are then puréed to make
a stunningly vibrant
sauce. It's especially
good served with
tagliatelle, tossed in a
little butter.

1 small **onion**, chopped,
or 30 ml/2 tbsp **frozen diced
onion**

100 ml/3½ fl oz/scant ½ cup very
hot (not boiling) **chicken stock**

1 large red (bell) **pepper** or
150 g/5 oz **frozen red and
yellow pepper slices**

1 **garlic clove**, crushed, or
2.5 ml/½ tsp **garlic purée** (paste)

60 ml/4 tbsp **dry white wine**,
orange juice or extra **chicken
stock**

200 g/7 oz/small can of **chopped
tomatoes**

**Salt and freshly ground black
pepper**

1 **bay leaf**

2 skinless **chicken breast fillets**

1   Put the onion in the ceramic cooking pot. Pour the stock over, cover with the lid and switch on the slow cooker to Auto. Leave to warm for 3–4 minutes while measuring and preparing the remaining ingredients.

2   If using a fresh pepper, halve, seed and roughly chop it. Stir the fresh or frozen pepper into the onion mixture with the garlic, wine or orange juice or extra stock, the tomatoes and salt and pepper. Add the bay leaf, then place the chicken breasts on top.

3   Cover with the lid and cook on Auto for 3–4 hours or on Low for 4–5 hours until the chicken and vegetables are cooked though and tender.

4   Remove the chicken breasts from the pot. Discard the bay leaf, then purée the sauce in a food processor or with a hand-held blender until smooth. Put one of the chicken breasts in a bowl or freezer container with half the sauce and leave to cool. Serve the remainder at once with tagliatelle or boiled or steamed rice.

Second serving

• Either cover the cooled chicken and chill in the fridge for the following day, or freeze for up to a month. If frozen, allow to defrost in the fridge overnight. To serve, heat gently in a saucepan, bubbling for a few minutes to ensure that the chicken is piping hot.

Cook's tip

• Frozen pepper slices are usually a mixture of red, yellow and green peppers. For this recipe use just the red and yellow ones.

jambalaya

Chef's note

Jambalaya is a rice, meat and seafood dish from Louisiana. Like so many recipes from the Deep South, cooking begins with the so-called 'trinity' of onion, green pepper and celery. The name is a linking of jambon, the French word for ham (a spicy sausage of some sort is always included) and alaya, meaning rice in an African dialect.

1

**1 - 1½ hrs
LOW**

Complete meal in itself

1 small **onion**, chopped, or 30 ml/2 tbsp **frozen diced onion**

1 **garlic clove**, crushed, or 5 ml/1 tsp **garlic purée** (paste)

1 **celery stick**, thinly sliced

½ green (bell) **pepper**, seeded and sliced, or 50 g/2 oz **frozen sliced mixed peppers**

A pinch of crushed dried **chilli flakes** or 2.5 ml/½ tsp **chilli paste**

1 small skinless **chicken breast**, cut into chunks

250 ml/8 fl oz/1 cup very hot (not boiling) **vegetable** or **chicken stock**

75 g/3 oz/⅓ cup **easy-cook (converted) rice**

Salt and freshly ground black pepper

50 g/2 oz large peeled **cooked prawns** (shrimp), thawed if frozen

1 **pepperami sausage stick**, sliced

15 ml/1 tbsp fresh or frozen **chopped parsley**

1   Put the onion, garlic, celery, pepper slices and chilli in the ceramic cooking pot. Arrange the chicken chunks on top of the vegetables, then pour the stock over. Cover with the lid, switch on the slow cooker to High and leave to cook for 30 minutes.

2   Add the rice to the chicken and vegetables, stir well and season generously. Re-cover with the lid and cook for a further ¾–1 hour or until the rice is just tender.

3   Stir in the prawns, pepperami and parsley and cook for a final 10–15 minutes to heat them through. Taste and re-season, if necessary, then serve straight away.

Cook's tip
• Instead of using a stick of celery, season with celery salt rather than ordinary salt.

chicken meat balls with rice

2

1¼ hrs HIGH

Complete meal in itself

Chef's note

These mouthwatering meatballs are very quick to make. Cooked with rice and peas in a flavoursome tomato sauce, this is a complete meal in itself and needs no further accompaniments.

15 g/½ oz **crustless wholemeal bread**

15 ml/1 tbsp **milk**

200 g/7 oz/small can of **chopped tomatoes with herbs**

5 ml/1 tsp **sun-dried tomato purée** (paste)

1 small **garlic clove**, crushed, or 2.5 ml/½ tsp **garlic purée**

200 ml/7 fl oz/scant 1 cup very hot (not boiling) **chicken stock**

175 g/6 oz **minced (ground) chicken**

Salt and freshly ground black pepper

75 g/3 oz/⅓ cup **easy-cook (converted) rice**

25 g/1 oz/1 tbsp **frozen peas**

1   Tear the bread into tiny pieces and put in a bowl. Sprinkle the milk over and leave to soak for a few minutes. Meanwhile, put the tomatoes, tomato purée, garlic and stock in the ceramic cooking pot and switch on the slow cooker to High. Cover with the lid and cook for 15 minutes while preparing the meatballs.

2   Add the minced chicken to the soaked bread and season with salt and pepper. Mix thoroughly using your hands, then shape into 10 small balls. Stir the rice into the tomato mixture, then carefully drop the meatballs, one at a time, on top. Re-cover with the lid and cook for 45 minutes. Spread out the peas on a plate lined with kitchen paper (paper towels) to thaw.

3   Scatter the peas around the meatballs, re-cover the pot with the lid and cook for a further 15 minutes or until the meatballs are cooked through and the rice is tender.

4   Remove half the meatballs (but not the sauce and rice mixture as this will not reheat well) and set aside in a dish or freezer container to cool. Serve the rice and sauce and remaining meatballs at once.

Second serving

- Either cover the cooled meatballs and chill in the fridge for the following day, or freeze for up to month. If frozen, allow the meatballs to defrost in the fridge overnight. Reheat by gently frying in 5 ml/1 tsp of oil in a non-stick frying pan for about 5 minutes, turning frequently until browned and heated through. To make a simple stroganoff sauce, sprinkle the meatballs with 1.5 ml/¼ tsp of ground paprika and add 60 ml/4 tbsp of crème fraîche and 30 ml/2 tbsp of stock to the pan. Season with salt and pepper and let the mixture bubble for a few minutes.

Cook's tip

- Minced turkey may be used instead of chicken.

hot and spicy mexican chicken

2

2-5 hrs
LOW

Rice, chopped avocado and soured (dairy sour) cream

Chef's note

Make the most of flavoured ingredients such as Mexican spice tomato purée (paste) as they make food preparation faster and simpler. Chicken thighs are an economical cut of chicken and have more flavour than breast (though two chicken breasts could be used here if you prefer). Buy the ready-skinned and boneless ones for this recipe.

---

1 small **onion**, thinly sliced, or 30 ml/2 tbsp **frozen diced onion**

250 ml/8 fl oz/1 cup very hot (not boiling) **chicken stock**

1 small red, yellow or green (bell) **pepper**, seeded and sliced, or 150 g/5 oz **frozen sliced peppers**

4 skinless, boneless **chicken thighs**

50 g/2 oz diced **chorizo sausage**

15 ml/1 tbsp **Mexican spice tomato purée** (paste)

Salt and freshly ground black pepper

1   Put the onion in the ceramic cooking pot and pour about half of the stock over. Cover with the lid and switch on the slow cooker to Auto or Low. Leave for a few minutes while measuring and preparing the rest of the ingredients.

2   Scatter the pepper slices over the onion. Cut the chicken thighs into 2.5 cm/1 in pieces and then place on top of the pepper with the chorizo. Blend the Mexican spice and tomato purée with the remaining stock, then stir in a little salt and pepper. Pour carefully over the chicken.

3   Cover with the lid and cook for 2–3 hours on Auto or 3–5 hours on Low or until the chicken and vegetables are very tender. Spoon half the chicken into a dish or freezer container and allow to cool. Serve the remainder at once with boiled or steamed rice and a side dish of chopped avocado and soured cream.

Second serving
- Either cover the cooled chicken and chill in the fridge for the following day, or freeze for up to a month. If frozen, allow to defrost in the fridge overnight. To serve, heat gently in a saucepan with an extra tablespoonful of water, allowing it to bubble for a few minutes to ensure that the chicken is piping hot.

Cook's tips
- Make this dish more substantial, if liked, by adding 45 ml/3 tbsp of canned red kidney or cannellini beans.
- If you can't find Mexican spice tomato purée, use sun-dried tomato purée instead and stir in a small pinch each of ground chilli, ground paprika, ground cumin and dried oregano or mixed herbs.

coq au vin

1

3-4 hrs
LOW

New, creamed or sautéed potatoes

Chef's note

This is a well-known French dish in which the chicken (originally an old cockerel) is marinated overnight in red wine to both tenderise the meat and give it extra flavour. It's an ideal way to use up that last bit of wine left in the bottle.

1 **chicken quarter**

100 ml/3½ fl oz/scant ½ cup **red wine**

1 small **onion**, chopped, or 30 ml/2 tbsp **frozen diced onion**

2.5 ml/½ tsp **garlic purée** (paste)

2.5 ml/½ tsp **dried thyme** or **mixed herbs**

75 ml/3 fl oz/5 tbsp very hot (not boiling) **chicken stock**

100 g/4 oz **baby button mushrooms** or **frozen whole or sliced mushrooms**

15 ml/1 tbsp fresh or frozen **chopped parsley**

Salt and freshly ground black pepper

1 Remove the skin from the chicken and place in a dish in which it fits fairly snugly. Pour the wine over. Cover tightly and marinate in the fridge for at least 4 hours or overnight.

2 Put the onion in the ceramic cooking pot. Add the garlic, herbs and stock and stir until blended. Add the mushrooms, followed by the chicken and the marinade.

3 Switch on the slow cooker to Auto, cover with the lid and cook for 3–4 hours or until the chicken is very tender and thoroughly cooked.

4 Transfer the chicken to a warm plate. Stir the parsley into the sauce and season to taste with salt and pepper. Pour over the chicken and serve at once with new, creamed or sautéed potatoes.

Cook's tip

• This dish is also good made with rosé or white wine instead of red. If liked, add a few fresh or frozen whole baby carrots and mini new potatoes to the cooking pot to make an all-in-one dish.

chicken and cashew biryani

1

1 - 1¼ hrs HIGH

Thick natural yoghurt and popadoms

Chef's note

This is a lightly spiced chicken and rice dish with golden caramelised onions and the added crunchy texture of cashew nuts. If you prefer, less expensive unsalted roasted peanuts may be used instead of the cashews.

½ × 400 g/14 oz/large can of **fried onions in olive oil**

1 small **garlic clove**, crushed, or 2.5 ml/½ tsp **garlic purée** (paste)

5 ml/1 tsp **curry paste**, preferably biryani

250 ml/8 fl oz/1 cup very hot (not boiling) **chicken stock**

175 g/6 oz **diced chicken breast** or 1 **chicken breast**, cut into thin strips

75 g/3 oz small florets of fresh or frozen **cauliflower**

50 g/2 oz/2 tbsp **frozen peas**

75 g/3 oz/⅓ cup **easy-cook (converted) basmati rice**

Salt and freshly ground black pepper

50 g/2 oz/½ cup **unsalted toasted cashew nuts**

30 ml/2 tbsp fresh or frozen **chopped coriander** (cilantro)

1   Put the onions, garlic and curry paste in the ceramic cooking pot. Pour in a small amount of the stock and stir until the curry paste is blended, then stir in the rest of the stock.

2   Add the chicken, cauliflower, peas and rice and season to taste with salt and pepper. Stir, then cover with the lid and switch on the slow cooker to High. Cook for 1–1¼ hours or until the chicken is cooked through and the rice is tender and has absorbed most of the stock.

3   Stir the nuts and coriander into the rice, then spoon on to a warm plate and serve straight away while hot, topped with a spoonful of thick natural yoghurt and accompanied by popadoms.

Cook's tips

- Use the other half of the canned onions in olive oil to make Cod with Onions and Capers (see pages 72–3).
- There are many different varieties of curry paste, which vary in flavour, heat and spiciness. These include:

Type	Main flavourings	Heat
Korma	Coconut and coriander	Mild
Tikka masala	Tomato and coconut	Medium
Balti	Tomato and coriander	Medium
Bhuna	Tomato and tamarind	Medium
Biryani	Coriander and cumin	Medium
Jalfrezi	Sweet pepper and coconut	Medium
Garam masala	Cinnamon and ginger	Hot
Madras	Cumin and chilli	Hot

chilli chicken and chorizo rice

1

1 - 1¼ hrs
HIGH

Complete meal in itself

Chef's note

This all-in-one dish is made using just a few simple ingredients. As it slowly cooks, the rice soaks up the flavour of the chorizo and the heat of the chilli mellows to make a wonderfully aromatic meal.

2 **shallots**, thinly sliced, or 30 ml/2 tbsp **frozen diced onion**

1 **garlic clove**, crushed, or 5 ml/1 tsp **garlic purée** (paste)

2.5 ml/½ tsp **chilli paste** or a pinch of crushed dried **chilli flakes**

1.5 ml/¼ tsp **dried mixed herbs**

250 ml/8 fl oz/1 cup very hot (not boiling) **chicken** or **vegetable stock**

150 g/5 oz **chicken breast, mini chicken fillets** or **ready-diced chicken**

50 g/2 oz **chorizo sausage** or **pepperami sausage**

75 g/3 oz/⅓ cup **easy-cook (converted) basmati rice**

50 g/2 oz **frozen mixed vegetables** or **peas**

Salt and freshly ground black pepper

1   Put the shallots or onion, garlic, chilli and herbs in the ceramic cooking pot.

2   Pour the stock over, cover with the lid and switch on the slow cooker to High. Cook for a few minutes while measuring and preparing the rest of the ingredients.

3   If the chicken isn't already diced, cut it into 2 cm/¾ in chunks and the chorizo into 1 cm/½ in pieces. Sprinkle the rice over the stock, then add the chicken, chorizo and mixed vegetables or peas. Season with salt and pepper, then give the mixture a stir.

4   Cover with the lid and cook for 1–1¼ hours or until the chicken and vegetables are cooked and the rice is tender and has absorbed most of the stock. Spoon on to a warm plate and serve at once.

Cook's tips

• If you prefer, leftover or ready-cooked chicken – or chopped cooked ham or prawns (shrimp) – can be used in this dish. Stir it into the rice mixture about 15 minutes before the end of the cooking time.
• Frozen mixed vegetables typically consist of diced carrots, sweetcorn and peas, but there are slightly more exotic versions available that also contain sliced red (bell) peppers, green beans and broccoli. Choose whichever you prefer.

poussin with pear stuffing

1

3-4 hrs
HIGH

New potatoes
and a green
vegetable

Chef's note

A whole poussin is perfect for a single serving and you can now buy them in all the major supermarkets. Here it is filled with a pear and sage stuffing that flavours the meat as it cooks and helps to keep it beautifully moist.

25 g/1 oz/2 tbsp **butter**

1 **shallot**, chopped, or 15 ml/1 tbsp **frozen diced onion**

1 firm **ripe pear**, cored, peeled and finely chopped

15 g/½ oz/¼ cup **fresh white breadcrumbs**

5 ml/1 tsp chopped **fresh sage** or 2.5 ml/½ tsp **dried sage**

Salt and freshly ground black pepper

1 **poussin** (Cornish hen), about 450 g/1 lb

A little **sunflower oil** for greasing

100 ml/3½ fl oz/scant ½ cup very hot (not boiling) **chicken stock**

Opposite: Poussin with Pear Stuffing (see above)

1 Melt the butter in a saucepan and stir in the shallot, pear, breadcrumbs, sage and salt and pepper. Lightly rinse the poussin inside and out, then pat dry on kitchen paper (paper towels). Spoon the stuffing into the cavity.

2 Lightly grease the base and half-way up the side of the ceramic cooking pot with oil.

3 Place the poussin in the pot and pour the stock over. Cover with the lid and switch on the slow cooker to High or Auto.

4 Cook for 3–4 hours or until the juices run completely clear when the poussin is pierced through the leg joint with a fine skewer. Turn off the slow cooker and leave the poussin to rest for 10 minutes before serving with new potatoes and a green vegetable.

Cook's tip

• If liked, make the cooking juices into a gravy to serve with the poussin. Tip the juices from the bottom of the cooking pot into a saucepan and skim off any excess fat. If necessary make it up to 150 ml/¼ pint/⅔ cup with extra stock. Blend 10 ml/2 tsp of cornflour (cornstarch) with 15 ml/1 tbsp of dry sherry or cold water and stir into the juices. Bring to the boil and simmer for 3–4 minutes until thickened and slightly reduced. Strain into a warm jug and serve.

Opposite: Duck with Orange Sauce (see pages 190–91)

honey mustard chicken

 **2**

 **2-3** hrs **HIGH**

 Mashed potatoes

Chef's note

A touch of curry powder lifts the flavours in this dish. I use Dijon mustard but any mild mustard will work.

225 g/8 oz skinless **chicken breast strips**

200 ml/8 fl oz/¾ cup hot **chicken stock**

1 **small onion**, chopped or 30 ml/2 tbsp **frozen diced onion**

1 **carrot**, sliced, or 75 g/3 oz **frozen sliced carrots**

15 ml/1 tbsp **honey**

7.5 ml/½ tbsp **Dijon mustard**

5 ml/1 tsp **curry powder**

5 ml/1 tsp **cornflour** (cornstarch)

30 ml/2 tbsp **water**

Salt and freshly ground black pepper

1   Put all the ingredients in the slow cooker and stir well.

2   Cover with the lid and cook on High for 2–3 hours until tender and cooked through.

3   Season to taste with salt and pepper.

4   Serve with mashed potatoes.

Second serving

- Reheat until piping hot, stir in a spoonful of mango chutney and serve with boiled rice.

caribbean-style chicken

2

3 hrs HIGH

Boiled rice

Chef's note

We usually expect cinnamon and cloves in a sweet dish but they add just a hint of Caribbean flavour to this simple dish.

225 g/8 oz skinless **chicken breast strips**

150 ml/¼ pt/⅔ cup hot **chicken stock**

400 g/14 oz/large can **black-eyed beans**, rinsed and drained

120 ml/4 fl oz/½ cup **passata** (sieved tomatoes)

1 **onion**, chopped or 45 ml/3 tbsp **frozen diced onion**

⅓ cup **frozen sliced peppers**

1 **garlic clove**, crushed or 5 ml/1 tsp **garlic purée** (paste)

A pinch of **ground cinnamon**

A pinch of **ground cloves**

30 ml/2 tbsp **rum**

Salt and cayenne pepper

1 Put all the ingredients except the rum, salt and cayenne pepper in the slow cooker and stir well.

2 Cover with the lid and cook on High for 2–3 hours.

3 Stir in the rum. Season to taste with salt and cayenne pepper and cook for a further 30 minutes until cooked through and tender.

4 Serve half the chicken immediately with boiled rice.

Second serving

- Cover the cooled chicken and chill in the fridge for the next day. Reheat until piping hot and serve with wraps and a green salad.

Cook's tips

- Try using turkey instead of chicken for a change.
- Black-eyed beans are also used in Chilli with Chorizo (see pages 142–3).

thai turkey curry

1

3-5 hrs LOW

Naan bread

Chef's note

Once it was only possible to make authentic-tasting curries with a huge number of different ingredients. Flavour-packed spice pastes have simplified curry cooking as this hot, yet creamy turkey dish shows.

25 g/1 oz **creamed coconut**, roughly chopped

200 ml/7 fl oz/scant 1 cup very hot (not boiling) **chicken** or **vegetable stock**

10 ml/2 tsp **Thai green curry paste**

4 **spring onions** (scallions), diagonally sliced

5 ml/1 tsp **lemon juice**

1 **turkey breast fillet** or **steak**, about 150 g/5 oz

100 g/4 oz **new potatoes**

50 g/2 oz/2 tbsp **frozen peas**

Salt and freshly ground black pepper

15 ml/1 tbsp fresh or frozen **chopped coriander** (cilantro)

1   Put the creamed coconut in the ceramic cooking pot and pour the stock over. Stir until the coconut has dissolved, then stir in the curry paste, spring onions and lemon juice.

2   Cover with the lid and switch on the slow cooker to Low. Leave for a few minutes while measuring and preparing the rest of the ingredients.

3   Cut the turkey into thin strips and the potatoes into chunks. Add them to the pot with the peas and season with salt and pepper. Cover and cook for 3–5 hours or until the turkey and vegetables are tender.

4   Taste and re-season, if necessary, then stir in the coriander. Serve on a warm plate with warmed naan bread.

Cook's tips

- Thai green curry paste contains an array of spices including green chillies, onions, garlic, lemon grass, galangal, coriander, cumin and tamarind.
- This curry can also be made with chicken breast or mini chicken breast fillets, pork fillet or lean rump steak.

turkey and bean cassoulet

2

3-5 hrs
LOW

Complete meal
in itself

A warming combination
of lean turkey, spicy
sausage and beans
makes this version
of the country dish
from south-west France a
hearty main meal.
It is served, as is
traditional, with a crisp
breadcrumb topping.

1 small **onion**, chopped,
or 30 ml/2 tbsp **frozen diced
onion**

1 small **garlic clove**, crushed, or
2.5 ml/½ tsp **garlic purée** (paste)

5 ml/1 tsp **sun-dried tomato
purée** (paste)

A pinch of **dried thyme** or **mixed
herbs**

150 ml/¼ pint/⅔ cup very hot (not
boiling) **chicken** or **vegetable
stock**

225 g/8 oz thinly cut lean **turkey
steaks**

50 g/2 oz coarse-cut dry-cured
French sausage, diced

400 g/14 oz/large can of **mixed
beans**, drained and rinsed

200 g/7 oz/small can of
tomatoes, preferably with basil

15 ml/1 tbsp **olive oil**

25 g/1 oz/½ cup fresh **white** or
wholemeal breadcrumbs

**Salt and freshly ground black
pepper**

1   Put the onion in the ceramic cooking pot. Blend together the garlic, tomato purée, herbs and about half the chicken stock, pour over the onion and switch on the slow cooker to Low. Leave to warm for a few minutes while measuring and preparing the rest of the ingredients.

2   Cut the turkey steaks into strips about 2 cm/¾ in wide. Add to the pot with the diced sausage and the beans. Mix together the remaining stock and the tomatoes and pour over. Cover and cook for 3–5 hours or until the turkey and onions are very tender.

3   Towards the end of the cooking time, heat the oil in a frying pan until hot. Add the breadcrumbs and cook, stirring constantly, for 3–4 minutes until lightly browned and crisp.

4   Season the cassoulet to taste with salt and pepper. Spoon half into a bowl or freezer container and leave to cool. Spoon the rest on to a warm serving plate and sprinkle the browned breadcrumbs over. Serve straight away.

Second serving

• Either cover the cooled cassoulet and chill in the fridge for the following day, or freeze for up to a month. If frozen, allow to defrost in the fridge overnight. To serve, heat gently in a saucepan with an extra tablespoonful of stock or water and allow to bubble for about 5 minutes.

Cook's tip

• Make a crunchy garlic bread topping for the second serving. Reheat the cassoulet in a heatproof casserole dish (Dutch oven), then top with 3 thin slices of French bread, lightly toasted and spread with 15 g/½ oz/1 tbsp of butter blended with 1 small crushed garlic clove or 2.5 ml/½ tsp of garlic purée. Cook under a moderate grill (broiler) for a few minutes until lightly browned and crisp.

comforting turkey casserole

2

3-4 hrs
LOW

New potatoes

Chef's note

You can vary the ingredients to suit what you have in the cupboard so this is a great basic recipe, especially good for winter fare.

225 g/8 oz diced **turkey breast**

200 g/7 oz/1 small can **chicken broth**

1 **small onion**, chopped or 30 ml/2 tbsp **frozen diced onions**

6 **button mushrooms**

5 ml/1 tsp **dried thyme**

A pinch of **celery seeds**

30 ml/2 tbsp **frozen peas**

200 g/7 oz/1 cup **frozen mixed vegetables**

Salt and freshly ground black pepper

1   Combine all the ingredients except the peas, vegetables, salt and pepper, cover with the lid and cook on LOW for 3–4 hours.

2   Turn the slow cooker to High and add the remaining ingredients, seasoning to taste.

3   Cook for a further 30 minutes until cooked through.

4   Serve with new potatoes.

Second serving

- Reheat the casserole in a flameproof dish until piping hot, top with mashed potato and grated cheese and brown under a hot grill for a few minutes until crisp.

turkey cacciatore

1

2-3 hrs HIGH

Cooked pasta or rice

Chef's note

A turkey breast cutlet, also known as a 'turkey steak' is a slice of skinless, boneless turkey breast, usually weighing around 175 g/ 6 oz. Turkey is very economical so it is a good choice for many dishes.

2 **turkey breast cutlets**, about 175 g/6 oz

200 g/7 oz/1 small can **chopped tomatoes**

30 ml/2 tbsp **water** or **wine**

2 **button mushrooms**, sliced

Pinch of **dried oregano**

1 small **courgette** (zucchini) sliced

Salt and freshly ground black pepper

1   Combine all the ingredients in the slow cooker except the courgette, salt and pepper.

2   Cover with the lid and cook on High for 2 hours.

3   Add the courgette and season with salt and pepper. Continue to cook for a further 30 minutes to 1 hour until cooked through and tender.

4   Serve with cooked pasta or rice.

Cook's tip
• Another tasty accompaniment would be some slices of garlic bread and a green salad.

duck with orange sauce

1

3-5 hrs **LOW**

Wholemeal toast or crusty bread rolls

Chef's note

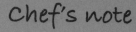

Briefly marinating the duck breast lets all the flavours penetrate the meat. However, don't worry if you haven't time – the duck will still be tender and delicious. If liked, serve with a green vegetable such as fine French beans, sugar snaps or mangetout (snow peas).

1 **orange**

5 ml/1 tsp **chilli oil**

1 skinless, boneless **duck breast**, about 175 g/6 oz

1 small **onion**, thinly sliced, or 30 ml/2 tbsp **frozen diced onion**

1 **celery stick**, sliced

100 g/4 oz **small new potatoes**, scrubbed and halved

150 ml/¼ pint/⅔ cup very hot (not boiling) **chicken** or **vegetable stock**

Salt and freshly ground black pepper

15 ml/1 tbsp fresh or frozen **chopped parsley** (optional)

1 Finely grate the zest from the orange. Squeeze the juice from the orange and whisk in a jug with the chilli oil and zest. Put the duck breast in a dish in which it fits snugly, then pour the orange juice mixture over. Cover with clingfilm (plastic wrap) and marinate in the fridge for an hour, or overnight if preferred.

2 When you are ready to cook, remove the duck from the fridge and allow it to come to room temperature. Meanwhile, put the onion, celery, potatoes and stock in the ceramic cooking pot and switch on to Low.

3 Put the duck on top of the vegetables. Season the marinade with a little salt and pepper and pour over. Cover and cook for 3–5 hours or until the duck and vegetables are tender.

4 Remove the duck from the slow cooker and leave on a board for a few minutes to 'rest', then cut into diagonal slices and arrange on a warm plate. Spoon the vegetables and sauce on to the plate and serve straight away, sprinkled with the parsley, if liked.

Cook's tips

- If you haven't any chilli oil, use sunflower oil instead and add a small pinch of crushed dried chilli flakes.
- Buy an unwaxed orange, if possible, as the skin will be free of preservatives.

vegetarian

You don't have to be a vegetarian to enjoy the occasional meat- or fish-free meal, as these delicious dishes show. Here you'll find recipes that make use of all kinds of wonderful ingredients from beans and pulses to grains and pasta. Many are based on vegetables that retain their shape and texture beautifully in the slow cooker. There are plenty of familiar favourites such as Cheese and Lentil Loaf (see pages 200–201) and Easy Vegetable Lasagne (see pages 214–15) and more unusual recipes from different cuisines that are destined to become your new favourites.

vegetarian tips

- If you don't eat meat, there are lots of other protein sources such as nuts and pulses. But do make sure that you get plenty of vitamins and minerals in your diet, including iron – as well as eggs, if you eat dairy, other non-meat sources of this vital mineral include dried fruit such as apricots and fortified breakfast cereals.

- These recipes may contain dairy products, which can sometimes be omitted or replaced with a vegan alternative, if preferred.

- Recipes may also use processed foods. Vegetarians should check the specific product labels to be certain of their suitability, especially items such as pastry, breads, stock, stock cubes and sauces.

- Some alcoholic drinks, including wine also use animal-derived products in their production.

- If you do eat dairy products, eggs make the ultimate simple meal for one and can easily be cooked in the slow cooker without the need to watch over them while they cook; try making Egg, Lentil and Coconut Curry (see pages 196–7).

- Eggs can usually be kept for up to 3 weeks (check the 'use by' date), so make great fridge fodder.

cheese and cannellini bake

2

3-4 hrs **HIGH**

Freshly cooked vegetables or salad

A little **oil** for greasing

1 slice of **white bread**, crusts removed

1 large **egg**, lightly beaten

30 ml/2 tbsp **vegetable stock**

400 g/14 oz/large can of **cannellini beans**, drained

1 small **onion**, roughly chopped, or 30 ml/2 tbsp **frozen diced onion**

1 **garlic clove**, roughly chopped, or 2.5 ml/½ tsp **garlic purée** (paste)

1 **celery stick**, roughly chopped

75 g/3 oz/¾ cup grated **mature Cheddar cheese**

30 ml/2 tbsp fresh or frozen **chopped parsley**

Salt and freshly ground black pepper

1   Place an upturned saucer or a metal pastry (paste) cutter in the base of the ceramic cooking pot. Pour in about 5 cm/2 in of hot (not boiling) water, then turn on the slow cooker to High. Grease a 13–15 cm/5–6 in round fixed-base cake tin or soufflé dish and line the base with greaseproof (waxed) paper or baking parchment.

2   Tear the bread into small pieces and put in a food processor. Pour the beaten egg and stock or milk over the bread and let it soak and soften for a minute.

3   Add the beans to the food processor with the onion, garlic and celery. Process until fairly smooth, then add the cheese, parsley and salt and pepper and process for a few more seconds or until everything is well-blended. Spoon and scrape the mixture into the prepared tin or dish, level the top, then cover with clingfilm (plastic wrap) or lightly oiled foil.

4   Place on top of the saucer or pastry cutter in the pot and pour in enough boiling water to come about half-way up the side of the tin or dish. Cover with the lid and cook for 3–4 hours or until firm and a skewer inserted into the middle comes out hot.

5   Carefully remove and leave for 5 minutes before turning out. If serving hot, cut in half and serve at once with freshly cooked vegetables. If serving cold, leave to cool completely and chill before slicing and serving with salad.

Second serving

• Put the remaining bake on a plate and cover with foil or clingfilm. Keep in the fridge for up to 3 days. This dish is not suitable for freezing.

egg, lentil and coconut curry

1

1½ hrs HIGH

Naan bread

Chef's note

Sometimes referred to as continental lentils, 'green' and 'brown' lentils have a distinctive disc shape that they retain when cooked. Here they are simmered in a coconut-curry sauce and served with a poached egg.

V

Suitable for vegetarians

50 g/2 oz **creamed coconut**

600 ml/1 pint/2½ cups very hot (not boiling) **vegetable stock**

1 small **onion**, chopped, or 30 ml/2 tbsp **frozen diced onion**

1 **garlic clove**, crushed, or 2.5 ml/½ tsp **garlic purée** (paste)

15 ml/1 tbsp **korma curry paste**

75 g/3 oz **green** or **brown lentils**

Salt and freshly ground black pepper

1 **egg**

1   Roughly chop the creamed coconut and put in the ceramic cooking pot. Pour the stock over and stir until the coconut has dissolved. Add the onion, garlic and curry paste. Switch on the slow cooker to Low.

2   Put the lentils in a sieve and rinse under cold running water. Allow to drain well, then add to the pot. Season with freshly ground black pepper (don't add any salt at this stage), stir, then cover with the lid and cook for 1¼ hours or until the lentils are just tender and have absorbed most of the liquid.

3   Season the lentils with a little salt, then make a small hollow in the middle. Break the egg on to a saucer, then gently tip into the hollow. Re-cover with the lid and cook for a further 15 minutes or until the egg white is set and the yolk is still soft, or a little longer if you prefer the egg firmer.

4   Carefully spoon half the curry mixture and the egg on to a warm serving plate. Season with salt and freshly ground black pepper and serve at once with some warmed naan bread.

Second serving

• Transfer the remaining curry to a bowl and leave to cool, then cover and chill in the fridge for the following day, or spoon into a freezer container and freeze for up to a month. If frozen, allow to defrost in the fridge overnight. Reheat in a saucepan with an extra tablespoonful of stock until hot and bubbling. Serve topped with thick natural yoghurt.

Cook's tip

• Don't add salt to lentils or pulses while cooking as it toughens them and they will take longer to cook.

chilli baked beans

2

2¼ hrs HIGH

Complete meal in itself

1 small **red onion**, finely chopped, or 30 ml/2 tbsp **frozen diced onion**

1.5 ml/¼ tsp crushed dried **chilli flakes**

A pinch of **ground cumin**

5 ml/1 tsp **sun-dried tomato purée** (paste)

100 ml/3½ fl oz/scant ½ cup very hot (not boiling) **vegetable stock**

200 g/7 oz/small can of **baked beans**

60 ml/4 tbsp canned **red kidney beans**, drained and rinsed

For the cornbread topping:

75 g/3 oz/¾ cup **cornmeal**

10 ml/2 tsp **wholemeal** or **plain (all-purpose) flour**

2.5 ml/½ tsp **baking powder**

Salt and freshly ground black pepper

1 **egg**, lightly beaten

45 ml/3 tbsp **milk**

1 Put the onion in the ceramic cooking pot with the chilli flakes, cumin and tomato purée and pour the stock over. Stir in the baked beans and kidney beans. Cover and switch on the slow cooker to Low or High. Cook for 1 hour on High or for 1½ hours on Auto.

2 Turn up the slow cooker to High. To make the cornbread topping, put the cornmeal, flour and baking powder in a bowl. Add salt and pepper, then stir together and make a hollow in the middle.

3 Add the egg and milk to the dry ingredients, then whisk together with a fork. Gradually mix everything together to make a stiff batter. Spoon over the bean mixture and cook for a further 45 minutes or until the topping is well risen and firm.

4 Spoon half the chilli baked beans and cornbread topping into a heatproof dish and leave to cool. Serve the rest at once.

Second serving
• Cover the cooled dish and chill in the fridge for the following day. Cover with foil and reheat in a moderate oven, or cover with clingfilm (plastic wrap) and microwave until hot.

cheese and lentil loaf

2

3 hrs LOW

Tomato sauce or pickles and a salad

Chef's note

Puy lentils are tiny dark-green marbled lentils and are considered to be superior in taste and texture to other varieties. Here, a ready-cooked sachet is turned into a pâté-like loaf. It is delicious served warm with a tomato salsa, or cold with pickles and a salad.

V
Suitable for Vegetarians

A little **oil** for greasing

4 **spring onions** (scallions), trimmed and roughly chopped

1 **carrot**, roughly chopped, or 75 g/3 oz **frozen sliced carrots**

1 **celery stick**, roughly chopped (optional)

60 ml/4 tbsp **vegetable stock**

1 **egg**

250 g/9 oz sachet of **cooked Puy lentils**

75 g/3 oz/¾ cup grated **Cheddar cheese**

2.5 ml/½ tsp **dried mixed herbs**

Salt and freshly ground black pepper

1 Put an upturned saucer or metal pastry (paste) cutter in the base of the ceramic cooking pot. Pour in about 5 cm/2 in of hot (not boiling) water, then turn on the slow cooker to Low. Grease a 13–15 cm/5–6 in round fixed-base cake tin or soufflé dish and line the base with greaseproof (waxed) paper or baking parchment.

2 Put the spring onions, carrot, celery and vegetable stock in a food processor and blend for a few seconds. Add the egg and blend again until the vegetables are finely chopped. Add the lentils, cheese, herbs and salt and pepper and blend again until everything is just mixed together (the mixture should still be a bit chunky, not completely smooth).

3 Spoon and scrape the mixture into the prepared tin or dish and level the top. Cover with lightly greased foil and place on top of the saucer or pastry cutter in the pot. Pour in enough boiling water to come half-way up the side of the dish or tin.

4 Cover with the lid and cook for 3 hours or until the loaf is lightly set and a skewer inserted into the middle comes out clean. Remove from the pot and leave to stand for a few minutes before turning out and slicing. Leave half the slices to cool and serve the other half with tomato sauce or pickles and a salad.

Second serving
• Either cover the cooled loaf slices and chill in the fridge for the following day, or wrap in greaseproof (waxed) paper and foil and freeze for up to a month. If frozen, allow to defrost in the fridge overnight. Either serve cold or reheat for 2 minutes in the microwave.

Cook's tip
• Make sure that the cheese you use is suitable for vegetarians.

wild mushroom risotto

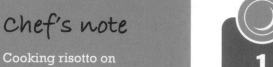

1 hr HIGH

Grated Parmesan cheese

Chef's note

Cooking risotto on the hob involves constant stirring, which is both time-consuming and tedious. In the slow cooker, the stock can be added all at once, and then the risotto left to cook with minimal attention.

V

Suitable for vegetarians

15 g/½ oz **dried porcini mushrooms**

200 ml/7 fl oz/scant 1 cup very hot (not boiling) **vegetable stock**

1 small **onion**, chopped, or 30 ml/2 tbsp **frozen diced onion**

10 g/¼ oz/small knob of **butter**

50 g/2 oz/¼ cup **Italian arborio (risotto) rice**

50 g/2 oz sliced fresh or frozen **button mushrooms**

Salt and freshly ground black pepper

15 ml/1 tbsp fresh or frozen **chopped parsley**

1   Put the porcini mushrooms in a heatproof bowl and pour over about half the stock. Put the onion and butter in the ceramic cooking pot, pour the rest of the stock over and switch on the slow cooker to High. Cover with the lid and leave for a few minutes while measuring and preparing the rest of the risotto ingredients.

2   Line a sieve (strainer) with a sheet of kitchen paper (paper towel) and place it over a jug. Drain the porcini mushrooms, reserving the stock. Snip them into smaller pieces with kitchen scissors and add them together with the stock to the pot. Stir in the rice and sliced mushrooms and season with salt and pepper.

3   Cook for 50–60 minutes, stirring once half-way through the cooking time. Stir in the parsley, then switch off the slow cooker and leave the risotto to stand for 2 minutes.

4   Gently stir, then spoon on to a warm plate or bowl and sprinkle with some Parmesan. Serve straight away.

Cook's tips

- For extra flavour, substitute a few spoonfuls of white wine, sherry or dry Madeira for part of the stock.
- Buy 'freshly grated' Parmesan or ready-prepared Parmesan shavings; they have an infinitely better flavour than the little tubs of powdery grated Parmesan cheese.
- Dried porcini mushrooms have a rich, intense flavour and are a useful standby to keep in your storecupboard. They should always be soaked in hot water for a few minutes to soften them and to remove any grit.

risotto verde

1

1 hr
LOW

Grated or shaved Parmesan

Chef's note

A good risotto, which is creamy and moist with tender grains that retain a slight bite, is easy to make in the slow cooker. This is a classic early summer dish, with a lovely fresh flavour. By using canned asparagus and frozen broad beans, as here, this delightful meal can be enjoyed all year round.

V
Suitable for Vegetarians

10 g/¼ oz/small knob of **butter**

4 **spring onions** (scallions), trimmed and sliced

50 g/2 oz/¼ cup **Italian arborio (risotto) rice**

60 ml/4 tbsp **dry white wine**

200 ml/7 fl oz/scant 1 cup boiling **vegetable stock**

Salt and freshly ground black pepper

100 g/4 oz **frozen broad (fava) beans**

400 g/14 oz/large can of **cut asparagus spears**, drained

1   Put the butter and spring onions in the ceramic cooking pot and switch on the slow cooker to High. Cover with the lid and leave for a few minutes or until the butter has melted while measuring and preparing the rest of the ingredients.

2   Stir the rice into the melted butter until all the grains are coated, then add the wine and stock. Season with salt and pepper, re-cover with the lid and cook for 45 minutes.

3   Meanwhile, spread out the broad beans on a plate to thaw and briefly rinse the asparagus spears under gently running cold water to remove the brine, then drain well.

4   Stir the rice, then gently stir in the broad beans and asparagus. Cover and cook for a further 15 minutes or until the rice is tender and has absorbed most of the liquid and the vegetables are piping hot. Switch off the slow cooker and leave the risotto to stand for 2 minutes.

5   Gently stir, then spoon on to a warm plate or bowl and sprinkle with some grated or shaved Parmesan. Serve straight away.

Cook's tips

• To make risotto, it is essential to use a short-grain rice. Arborio, which originates from the Po valley region in Italy, is the most widely sold variety of risotto rice, but you can also find varieties such as vialone, nano and carnaroli, which would all be suitable for this dish.
• Use a potato peeler to make Parmesan shavings.

spiced bean and pumpkin stew

2

4-5 hrs LOW

Crusty wholemeal bread

1 small **onion**, chopped, or 30 ml/2 tbsp **frozen diced onion**

1 **garlic clove**, crushed, or 5 ml/1 tsp **garlic purée** (paste)

5 ml/1 tsp **sweet paprika**

A pinch of crushed dried **chilli flakes** or 1.25 ml/¼ tsp **chilli paste**

120 ml/4 fl oz/½ cup very hot (not boiling) **vegetable stock**

350 g/12 oz peeled **pumpkin** or squash, cut into 2.5 cm/1 in cubes

225 g/8 oz peeled fresh or frozen **sweet potatoes**, cut into 2.5 cm/ 1 in cubes

100 g/4 oz trimmed **okra** (ladies' fingers) or fresh or frozen **French beans**

½ × 400 g/14 oz/large can of **cannellini** or **haricot (navy) beans**

120 ml/4 fl oz/½ cup **passata** (sieved tomatoes)

Salt and freshly ground black pepper

1   Put the onion, garlic, paprika and chilli in the ceramic cooking pot. Pour the stock over, cover with the lid and switch on the slow cooker to Low. Leave for 3–4 minutes while measuring and preparing the rest of the ingredients.

2   Add the pumpkin and sweet potato cubes, the okra or French beans and the cannellini or haricot beans. Pour the passata over and season with salt and pepper.

3   Stir everything together, then re-cover with the lid and cook for 4–5 hours or until the vegetables are very tender. Transfer half the stew to a bowl or freezer container and allow to cool.

4   Serve the remainder straight away on a warm plate, accompanied by crusty wholemeal bread.

Second serving
• Either cover the cooled mixture and chill in the fridge for the following day, or freeze for up to a month. If frozen, allow to defrost in the fridge overnight. To serve, transfer to a saucepan and heat until piping hot.

Cook's tip
• Use the remaining beans to make Chilli Bean Chowder (see pages 24–5) or Braised Lamb with Cannellini – a non-vegetarian recipe (see pages 114–15).

mauritian vegetable curry

2

3-5 hrs **LOW**

Rice or naan bread

1 small **onion**, chopped, or 30 ml/2 tbsp **frozen diced onion**

1 **garlic clove**, crushed, or 5 ml/1 tsp **garlic purée** (paste)

5 ml/1 tsp freshly grated **root ginger** or **ginger purée** (paste)

15 ml/1 tbsp **medium curry powder**

A pinch of **ground turmeric**

2 fresh **curry leaves**

600 ml/1 pint/2½ cups hot (not boiling) **vegetable stock**

75 g/3 oz **potato**, peeled and cut into 1 cm/½ in cubes

75 g/3 oz **aubergine** (eggplant), cut into 1 cm/½ in cubes

1 **carrot**, cut into 1 cm/½ in dice, or 75 g/3 oz **frozen diced carrots**

75 g/3 oz fresh or frozen **green beans**

30 ml/2 tbsp fresh or frozen **chopped coriander** (cilantro)

Salt and freshly ground black pepper

1   Put the onion, garlic, ginger, curry powder, turmeric and curry leaves in the ceramic cooking pot. Pour the stock over, cover with the lid and switch on the slow cooker to Low. Leave for 4–5 minutes while measuring and preparing the remaining ingredients.

2   Add the potato, aubergine, carrot and beans. Re-cover with the lid and cook for 3–5 hours or until all the vegetables are tender.

3   Stir in the coriander, then season with salt and pepper. Transfer half the curry to a bowl or freezer container and allow to cool.

4   Serve the rest of the curry on a warm plate or bowl, accompanied by boiled or steamed rice or warmed naan bread.

Second serving

• Either cover the cooled curry and chill in the fridge for the following day, or freeze for up to a month. If frozen, allow to defrost in the fridge overnight. To serve, transfer to a saucepan and heat until piping hot.

Cook's tips

• Fresh curry leaves add a wonderful authentic aromatic flavour to this dish and can be frozen for future use. If you can't get any, add a couple of bay leaves instead.
• Serve the curry with some bought or home-made cucumber raita (see pages 124–5), or simply with a spoonful or two of thick natural yoghurt.

red lentil and vegetable dhal

 2

 3-5 hrs LOW

 Thick natural yoghurt and toasted flaked (slivered) almonds

Chef's note

A bag of frozen mixed grilled vegetables is a great buy! Slices of red and yellow (bell) pepper, courgette (zucchini) and aubergine (eggplant) are already lightly grilled, which brings out their flavour. Combined with spiced lentils, they make a wonderful vegetarian meal. A sprinkling of nuts adds both protein and texture.

V

Suitable for vegetarians

1 small **onion**, finely chopped, or 30 ml/2 tbsp **frozen diced onion**

1 **garlic clove**, crushed, or 5 ml/1 tsp **garlic purée** (paste)

15 ml/1 tbsp **curry paste**

400 ml/14 fl oz/1¾ cups very hot (not boiling) **vegetable stock**

50 g/2 oz/⅓ cup **red lentils**

½ × 750 g/1¾ lb bag of **frozen grilled (broiled) vegetables,** preferably thawed

Salt and freshly ground black pepper

1   Put the onion, garlic and curry paste in the ceramic cooking pot, add a little of the stock and stir thoroughly until the curry paste is well blended.

2   Add the remaining stock, the lentils and grilled vegetables. Stir to combine, then cover with the lid and switch on the slow cooker to Low.

3   Cook for 3–5 hours or until the lentils and vegetables are very tender. Season to taste with salt and pepper.

4   Spoon half the dhal into a dish and leave to cool. Serve the remaining dhal at once, drizzled with a little yoghurt and scattered with toasted flaked almonds.

Second serving
- Cover the cooled dhal and chill in the fridge for the following day. To serve, heat gently in a saucepan with an extra tablespoonful of stock or water until bubbling and hot.

Cook's tips
- You can use other frozen vegetables such as cauliflower, broccoli or cubed sweet potato for part or all of the grilled mixed vegetables.
- Frozen grilled vegetables are also used to make Grilled Vegetable Bake (see pages 52–3).

hot cashew and spinach rice

1

1-1¼ hrs
HIGH

Natural thick
yoghurt and
toasted unsalted
cashew nuts

Here's a colourful and
easy vegetarian dish that
makes a satisfying main
course all on its own.
Toasted cashew nuts add
extra protein as well a
lovely crunchy texture.

V

Suitable for
Vegetarians

1 small **onion**, chopped,
or 30 ml/2 tbsp **frozen diced
onion**

1 small **garlic clove**, crushed, or
2.5 ml/½ tsp **garlic purée** (paste)

5 ml/1 tsp **curry paste**

250 ml/8 fl oz/1 cup very hot (not
boiling) **vegetable stock**

75 g/3 oz/⅓ cup **easy-cook
(converted) rice**

100 g/4 oz **baby spinach leaves**

**Salt and freshly ground black
pepper**

1   Put the onion, garlic and curry paste in the ceramic cooking pot. Pour in a little of the stock and stir until blended, then stir in the rest of the stock. Stir in the rice, cover with the lid and turn on the slow cooker to High. Cook for 40 minutes.

2   Give the rice a stir, then lay the spinach on the surface of the rice. Season with salt and freshly ground black pepper. Replace the lid and cook for a further 20–30 minutes or until the spinach has wilted and the rice is cooked and tender.

3   Stir to mix the rice and spinach together, then taste and re-season, if necessary. Serve at once, topped with a spoonful of natural thick yoghurt and scattered with toasted cashew nuts.

Cook's tips

- Look for ready-toasted cashew nuts in the supermarket. If you can't get any, toast plain unsalted nuts in a small non-stick frying pan over a medium heat for 2–3 minutes, stirring frequently. Turn off the heat as soon as the nuts start to colour as they will continue cooking for a little while in the heat of the pan. Toasted flaked (slivered) almonds may be used instead of cashews, if preferred.
- If baby spinach leaves are unavailable, use ordinary spinach leaves or Swiss chard instead, removing any tough stalks and tearing the leaves into smaller pieces.

easy vegetable lasagne

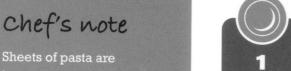

1

1 ¼-2 hrs
HIGH

A green salad

A little **olive oil** for greasing

400 g/14 oz/large can of **ratatouille**

3 sheets of no-need-to precook **lasagne**

½ × 400 g/14 oz jar of **white sauce**

25 g/1 oz/¼ cup grated **mature Cheddar cheese** or 15 g/½ oz/ 2 tbsp grated **Parmesan cheese**

1   Lightly grease the base and a third of the way up the side of the ceramic cooking pot with the oil. Spoon in half the ratatouille.

2   Top with a sheet of lasagne, breaking it to fit, if necessary. Stir the white sauce, then spoon half over the lasagne. Top with another sheet of lasagne.

3   Spoon the remaining ratatouille over, then top with the last sheet of lasagne. Finish with the rest of the white sauce, smoothing it level with the back of the spoon. Sprinkle the cheese over.

4   Cover with the lid and switch on the slow cooker to Auto or High for 1 hour, then leave on Auto or reduce the temperature to Low and cook for a further ¾–1 hour or until the lasagne is tender. Serve at once with a green salad.

Cook's tips

- Jars of white sauce are often labelled 'white lasagne sauce' and are subtly flavoured with herbs and sometimes Parmesan cheese. White sauce is also used to make Tuna Cannelloni (see pages 78–9). If you prefer to make your own all-in-one sauce instead, put 15 g/½ oz/ 1 tbsp of butter, 15 g/½ oz/2 tbsp of plain (all-purpose) flour and 150 ml/¼ pint/⅔ cup of milk in a saucepan. Bring to the boil over a medium heat, whisking all the time until thickened. Add a pinch of dried oregano or mixed herbs and season lightly with salt and freshly ground black pepper.
- For a browned top, place under a moderate (not hot, as this could crack the ceramic cooking pot) grill (broiler) for 2–3 minutes until golden brown and bubbling.
- Make the dish more substantial by stirring 50 g/2 oz of sliced fresh or frozen mushrooms or frozen peas into the ratatouille.

sweet and sour quorn

1

3-5 hrs **HIGH**

Noodles or rice

5 ml/1 tsp **cornflour** (cornstarch)

10 ml/2 tsp **dark soy sauce**

5 ml/1 tsp **balsamic vinegar**

5 ml/1 tsp **hoisin sauce**

5 ml/1 tsp **clear honey**

200 g/7 oz/small can of **pineapple pieces in juice**

100 g/4 oz frozen **chicken-style Quorn pieces**

¼ × 500 g/18 oz packet of **frozen 'Chinese wok' vegetables**

Salt and freshly ground black pepper

1   Put the cornflour in the ceramic cooking pot and add the soy sauce and balsamic vinegar. Stir together until blended, then stir in the hoisin sauce and honey.

2   Stir in the pineapple pieces and juice, followed by the Quorn and vegetables. Season with a little salt and pepper.

3   Cover with the lid and switch on the slow cooker to High or Auto. Cook for 3–5 hours or until the vegetables are tender.

4   Spoon on to a warm plate and serve straight away with noodles or rice.

Cook's tips

- Quorn pieces are made with mycoprotein, a member of the fungi family. Because it contains egg white, it is unsuitable for vegans.
- Frozen 'Chinese wok' vegetables are a mixture of beansprouts, carrots, sugar snap peas, water chestnuts, Chinese mushrooms, (bell) peppers, mustard green stems and ginger.

meat-free bolognese

 **2**

 **3-5** hrs **LOW**

 Spaghetti and grated vegetarian Parmesan cheese (optional)

Chef's note

This basic meat-free mince mixture is incredibly versatile and can be used as a basis for a number of other dishes. The recipe given here is for two portions but, if you have freezer space, it's well worth doubling the quantity.

V

Suitable for Vegetarians

1 small **onion**, chopped, or 30 ml/2 tbsp **frozen diced onion**

1 **garlic clove**, crushed, or 5 ml/1 tsp **garlic purée** (paste)

120 ml/4 fl oz/½ cup very hot (not boiling) **vegetable stock**

225 g/8 oz frozen **soya mince** or **'meat-free' mince**

1 **carrot**, finely chopped, or 75 g/3 oz **frozen diced carrots**

50 g/2 oz fresh or frozen **sliced mushrooms**

200 g/7 oz/small can of **chopped tomatoes**

5 ml/1 tsp **sun-dried tomato purée**

120 ml/4 fl oz/½ cup **red** or **white wine** or extra **vegetable stock**

2.5 ml/½ tsp **dried mixed herbs**

Salt and freshly ground black pepper

1   Put the onion and garlic in the ceramic cooking pot and pour the stock over. Cover with the lid and switch on the slow cooker to Auto or Low. Leave to cook for a few minutes while measuring and preparing the rest of the ingredients.

2   Add the mince, carrot, mushrooms, tomatoes, tomato purée, wine or extra stock and herbs to the pot. Season with salt and pepper. Stir well, then re-cover with the lid and cook for 3–5 hours or until the vegetables are very tender.

3   Spoon half the mince mixture into a bowl or freezer container and allow to cool. Serve the remainder as for Bolognese, spooned on top of cooked spaghetti or pasta. Sprinkle with freshly grated Parmesan, if liked.

Second serving

- Either cover the cooled mince and chill in the fridge for the following day, or freeze for up to a month. If frozen, allow the mince to defrost in the fridge overnight. To serve, heat gently in a saucepan and allow to bubble for about 5 minutes until piping hot.

mixed bean hotpot

1

4-6 hrs **LOW**

Complete meal in itself

Chef's note

This easy one-pot dish of beans and vegetables makes a nourishing winter main course and needs no accompaniments. The combination of sugar, wine vinegar and passata gives it a tasty sweet and sour flavour.

2.5 ml/½ tsp **light brown sugar**

5 ml/1 tsp **red wine vinegar**

5 ml/1 tsp **Worcestershire sauce** or **dark soy sauce**

1 small **garlic clove**, crushed, or 2.5 ml/½ tsp **garlic purée** (paste)

150 ml/¼ pint/⅔ cup **passata** (sieved tomatoes)

4 **spring onions** (scallions), trimmed and sliced

½ × 400 g/14 oz/large can of **mixed beans**, drained and rinsed

75 g/3 oz fresh or frozen **green beans**, trimmed if fresh and halved

75 g/3 oz fresh or frozen **sliced mushrooms**

150 g/5 oz **potato**, peeled and roughly cut into 2 cm/¾ in chunks

1.5 ml/¼ tsp **dried mixed herbs**

Salt and freshly ground black pepper

1   Put the sugar, wine vinegar, Worcestershire or soy sauce and garlic in the ceramic cooking pot. Add a little of the passata and stir until blended. Stir in the rest of the passata.

2   Add the spring onions, mixed beans, green beans, mushrooms, potato chunks and herbs. Season with salt and pepper, then stir everything together.

3   Cover with the lid and switch on the slow cooker to Auto or Low. Cook for 4–6 hours or until the vegetables are tender. Spoon on to a warm plate and serve straight away.

Cook's tip
• Transfer the remaining half-can of beans to a small container, cover and store in the fridge for up to 3 days, or freeze.

butter bean bake

2

3 hrs HIGH

Vegetables of your choice or salad

1 × 425 g/15 oz/large can of **butter (lima) beans**, drained and rinsed

30 ml/2 tbsp **milk**

4 **spring onions** (scallions), trimmed and sliced

25 g/1 oz/½ cup fresh **brown breadcrumbs**

30 ml/2 tbsp **chopped fresh parsley**

10 ml/2 tsp **dried sage**

1 **egg**, lightly beaten

50 g/2 oz/½ cup grated **Cheddar cheese**

30 ml/2 tbsp grated **Parmesan cheese**

Salt and freshly ground black pepper

Oil or **butter** for greasing

1   Place an upturned saucer or a metal pastry (paste) cutter in the bottom of the ceramic cooking pot. Pour in about 2.5 cm/1 in hot (not boiling) water and switch on the slow cooker to High.

2   Put the butter beans, milk and spring onions in a food processor and blend until fairly smooth. Transfer the mixture to a bowl, then add all the remaining ingredients and mix thoroughly. Spoon into a greased and lined 450 g/1 lb loaf tin or soufflé dish, level the top and cover with clingfilm (plastic wrap).

3   Place in the slow cooker and pour in enough boiling water to come two-thirds of the way up the sides of the tin or dish. Cover with the lid and cook for 3 hours or until firm and a skewer inserted into the middle comes out hot.

4   Carefully remove from the slow cooker and place on a wire cooling rack. Leave for 5 minutes before turning out.

5   If serving hot, cut off two thick slices and serve at once with fresh vegetables. If serving cold, leave to cool completely and chill before slicing.

Second serving

- Wrap the remaining Butter Bean Bake in clingfilm and keep in the fridge for 2 days.

mediterranean vegetable stew

2

3-5 hrs
LOW

Rice or French
bread

Chef's note

This is a tasty way to ensure that you're eating a wide variety of fresh vegetables. You could add extra protein by sprinkling the stew with some toasted pine nuts or grated Parmesan cheese just before serving, but it is also good as a vegetable dish in its own right.

V

Suitable for
vegetarians

1 **garlic clove,** crushed,
or 5 ml/1 tsp **garlic purée**
(paste)

400 g/14 oz/large can or carton
of **chopped tomatoes with basil
and onion**

175 g/6 oz **aubergine** (eggplant),
cut into 2 cm/¾ in cubes

1 red or yellow (bell) **pepper,**
halved, seeded and sliced,
or 150 g/5 oz **frozen mixed
pepper slices**

100 g/4 oz sliced fresh or frozen
button mushrooms

**Salt and freshly ground black
pepper**

1   Blend the garlic with a little of the tomatoes in the ceramic cooking pot, then stir in the remainder. Add the aubergine, sliced pepper and mushrooms and a little salt and pepper.

2   Cover with the lid and cook on Low for 3–5 hours or until all the vegetables are tender and the sauce has thickened. Taste and re-season, if necessary.

3   Spoon half the vegetable mixture into a bowl and leave to cool. Spoon the rest on to a warm serving plate and serve straight away with boiled or steamed rice or crusty French bread.

Second serving

- Cover the cooled vegetable stew and chill in the fridge for the following day. To serve, heat gently in a saucepan and allow to bubble for a few minutes until piping hot. This dish is not suitable for freezing.

desserts & cakes

A pot of yoghurt or some fresh fruit is a simple and healthy way to end a meal, but sometimes you may feel like something a little more indulgent. From light fruit compôtes to creamy baked custards and decadent chocolate puddings, you'll find all manner of desserts here to suit every season and occasion. Try classic favourites such as Chocolate Rice Pudding (see pages 230–31) or Rich Christmas Pudding (see pages 240–41), or indulge yourself with Double Chocolate Cake (see pages 246–7) or Blueberry Panettone (see pages 234–5). There's plenty of choice to satisfy anyone with a sweet tooth.

Many cakes can be made successfully in a slow cooker. Moist mixtures such as Dark and Sticky Gingerbread (see pages 244–5) work especially well as they require long cooking at a low temperature. These types of cake are usually allowed to mature before eating, but this isn't necessary when they are made in the slow cooker.

The cakes suggested here are all small-sized ones that cut into four slices and may be frozen. Some are covered with delicious frostings but, if you prefer, you can finish them by sprinkling with a few chopped or flaked nuts before cooking, or by simply dusting with icing (confectioners') sugar afterwards.

desserts & cakes

desserts & cakes tips

- If you use dried fruit, make sure it is covered with liquid in order to cook evenly.

- If you are steaming puddings, fill the basins two-thirds full and make a pleat in the greaseproof (waxed) paper to allow space for the pudding to rise. Pour very hot (not boiling) water around the puddings to start them off well, and cook them on High.

- When adapting your own recipes, remember that fruit will require less cooking liquid.

cherry custard pots

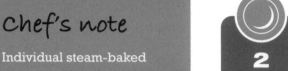 

2

2-3 hrs **LOW**

Chef's note

Individual steam-baked vanilla custards make great warm or chilled desserts. Spoon a little fruit conserve or compôte into the base – cherry conserve is suggested here for a lovely summer-fruit flavour. The custards should be a little wobbly when they first come out of the slow cooker as the mixture will thicken as it cools.

V

Suitable for Vegetarians

150 ml/¼ pint/⅔ cup **milk**

75 ml/3 fl oz/5 tbsp **double (heavy) cream**

A little softened **butter** for greasing

30 ml/2 tbsp **cherry conserve**

15 ml/1 tbsp **caster (superfine) sugar**

2.5 ml/½ tsp **vanilla essence (extract)**

1 **egg**

1 Pour about 4 cm/1½ in of very hot (not boiling) water into the base of the ceramic cooking pot and switch on the slow cooker to Low. Pour the milk and cream into a jug and stand in the hot water to allow it to warm a little.

2 Meanwhile, lightly grease two 150 ml/¼ pint/⅔ cup ramekins (custard cups) with butter. Spoon in the conserve, dividing it equally between them.

3 Beat together the caster sugar, vanilla extract and egg in a bowl until blended. Pour the milk and cream over the egg mixture, beating well. Divide between the ramekins, cover with clingfilm (plastic wrap) and place in the pot.

4 Cover with the lid and cook for 2–3 hours or until lightly set. Carefully remove from the pot and leave to stand for a few minutes. Either serve warm or leave to cool, then chill in the fridge for at least 1 hour.

Second serving
- If liked, turn the second serving into a cream brulée – but first make sure that the dish is heatproof. Sprinkle the top evenly with 30 ml/ 2 tbsp of golden caster sugar, then place under a preheated moderate grill (broiler) and cook until the sugar melts and caramelises. Allow to cool before serving.

Cook's tips
- Check that the ramekins will fit side by side in the slow cooker. If not, make the cherry custard in a single 300 ml/½ pint/1¼ cup dish
- For a less rich version, replace the cream with milk.

chocolate rice pudding

2

3-6 hrs
LOW

Chef's note

Because little liquid escapes from the slow cooker during cooking, this rich and creamy dessert is made from evaporated milk and unlike oven-cooked versions it doesn't form a thick skin on the top. A small amount of dark chocolate makes it a special treat.

V

Suitable for vegetarians

A little softened **butter** for greasing

15 ml/1 tbsp **cocoa (unsweetened chocolate) powder**

25 g/1 oz/2 tbsp **caster (superfine) sugar**

375 ml/13 fl oz/1½ cups **evaporated milk**

40 g/1½ oz **pudding rice**, rinsed and drained

25 g/1 oz **plain (semi-sweet) chocolate** squares or chips

1   Grease the base and about a third of the way up the side of the ceramic cooking pot with butter. Blend together the cocoa powder, sugar and about 45 ml/3 tbsp of the evaporated milk in the cooking pot, then when combined, gradually blend in the rest of the evaporated milk.

2   Add the rice and stir again, then cover with the lid. Cook on High for 3–4 hours or on Low for 6–8 hours, stirring once or twice during the final 2 hours. The pudding is ready when the rice is tender and has absorbed most of the milk.

3   Stir in the chocolate until melted, then spoon half the pudding into a bowl and leave to cool. Serve the rest straight away, while still hot in a bowl.

Second serving
• Cover the cooled pudding and chill in the fridge for the following day. Serve cold, or reheat gently in a saucepan until piping hot.

Cook's tips
• For a lighter, less rich pudding, make with part evaporated milk and part full-fat milk.
• For a plain rice pudding, leave out the cocoa and chocolate and sprinkle in a little freshly grated nutmeg towards the end of the cooking time. Serve drizzled with honey or with a spoonful of jam (jelly) or lemon curd in the centre.
• For caramel rice pudding, leave out the cocoa, chocolate and sugar and substitute 150 ml/¼ pint/⅔ cup crème de leche (caramel cream) for the same amount of evaporated milk.
• For bay-scented Italian rice pudding, leave out the cocoa and chocolate, use risotto rather than pudding rice and add a bay leaf.

chocolate pudding

2

2-3 hrs HIGH

For the chocolate pudding:

50 g/2 oz/¼ cup **butter**, softened, plus extra for greasing

50 g/2 oz/¼ cup **light brown sugar**

40 g/1½ oz **self-raising flour**

15 ml/1 tbsp **cocoa (unsweetened chocolate) powder**

1 **egg**, lightly beaten

10 ml/2 tsp **milk**

For the hot chocolate sauce:

15 g/½ oz/1 tbsp **butter**

75 g/3 oz **plain (semi-sweet) chocolate**, broken into squares, or **plain chocolate chips**

45 ml/3 tbsp **milk**

30 ml/2 tbsp **double (heavy) cream**

15 ml/1 tbsp **golden (light corn) syrup**

1. Place an upturned saucer or a metal pastry (paste) cutter in the base of the ceramic cooking pot. Pour in about 5 cm/2 in of hot (not boiling) water, then turn on the slow cooker to High.

2. To make the chocolate pudding, grease a 450 ml/¾ pint/2 cup pudding basin and line the base with a circle of greaseproof (waxed) paper or baking parchment.

3. Put the butter and sugar in a bowl and stir for a few seconds until mixed together. Sift in the flour and cocoa powder, then add the egg and milk and beat everything together for about 2 minutes until well mixed and light. Spoon and scrape the mixture into the prepared basin and smooth the top. Cover with clingfilm (plastic wrap) or lightly greased foil.

4. Place the pudding basin on top of the saucer or pastry cutter in the pot, then pour in enough boiling water to come two-thirds up the side of the basin. Cover with the lid and cook for 2–3 hours or until the sponge is well risen and firm to the touch. Carefully remove from the pot and leave, still covered, to stand for a few minutes while making the sauce.

5. To make the sauce, put all the ingredients in a heatproof bowl and place in the still-hot water in the ceramic cooking pot. Leave for 5 minutes or until the butter and chocolate have melted, then whisk the sauce until smooth. Turn out the pudding on to a warm plate, pour over the sauce and serve.

Cook's tips
- The pudding can be made up to the end of step 3 and left in a cool place for up to 2 hours before cooking.
- Reheat the second portion of the pudding in an overproof dish covered with foil in a low oven and the sauce in a bowl over a pan of hot water, or spoon the sauce over the pudding and reheat in the microwave.

blueberry panettone

2

3-5 hrs
HIGH

Whipped cream
or Greek-style
yoghurt

75 g/3 oz packet of **dried blueberries**

30 ml/2 tbsp **brandy** or **extra milk**

25 g/1 oz/2 tbsp **butter**, softened

150 g/5 oz **panettone**, cut into medium slices

1 small **egg**, lightly beaten

200 ml/7 fl oz/scant 1 cup **milk**

5 ml/1 tsp **caster (superfine) sugar**

1 Put the blueberries in a small bowl, pour the brandy or milk over and leave to soak for a few minutes. Place an upturned saucer or a metal pastry (paste) cutter in the base of the ceramic cooking pot and pour in about 2.5 cm/1 in of very hot (not boiling) water). Switch on the slow cooker to High.

2 Use about a third of the butter to grease the base and sides of a 600 ml/1 pint/2½ cup heatproof dish, about 5 cm/2 in deep (make sure first that it fits in the pot). Thinly spread the panettone slices with the remaining butter, then cut each slice diagonally into quarters. Arrange in the dish, scattering the blueberries between the layers.

3 Whisk together the egg, milk and any remaining soaking liquid. Pour the milk mixture slowly over the panettone, then gently press the panettone slices down into the liquid. Sprinkle the top with the sugar, then cover with clingfilm (plastic wrap) or lightly greased foil.

4 Place the dish on top of the saucer or pastry cutter in the pot, then pour in enough boiling water to come half-way up the side of the dish. Cover with the lid and cook for 3–5 hours or until the custard is lightly set.

5 Serve half the pudding hot with plenty of whipped cream or Greek-style yoghurt.

Second serving

- Allow the rest of the pudding to cool in the dish. Cover and chill in the fridge for the following day. Serve cold – do not reheat.

Cook's tips

- Use an orange liqueur instead of the brandy, if preferred.
- You'll find panettone in major supermarkets and delicatessens. Look for the tiny versions, which are ideal for this pudding.

tropical fruit salad

2

4-6 hrs LOW

Dried coconut shavings and Greek-style yoghurt

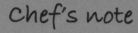

Chef's note

You can buy ready-to-eat dried exotic fruit in a single packet containing a mixture of papaya, pineapple, mango and melon or alternatively create your own combination by choosing your favourites. They are cooked slowly in pineapple juice, flavoured with lime and sweetened with honey to make a healthy dessert.

V

Suitable for Vegetarians

1 **lime**

300 ml/½ pint/1¼ cups **pineapple juice**

15 ml/1 tbsp **clear honey**

250 g/9 oz packet of **ready-to-eat dried exotic fruit**

1 Pare a long strip of zest from the lime and put it in the ceramic cooking pot with all the remaining ingredients. Cover with the lid and switch on the slow cooker to Low.

2 Cook for 4–6 hours or until the fruit is very tender and most of the fruit juice has been absorbed. Turn off the heat.

3 Halve the lime, squeeze out the juice and stir into the fruit salad. Leave the fruit salad to cool, then spoon half into a bowl and serve scattered with coconut shavings and with a spoonful of Greek-style yoghurt.

Second serving

- Transfer the remaining fruit salad to a bowl and leave to cool. Cover and chill in the fridge for the following day. Serve cold with ice-cream or at room temperature.

Cook's tips

- Adding the lime juice after cooking helps preserve the vitamin C, which could otherwise be destroyed by the long, slow cooking.
- Create a tropical fruit sundae by layering the fruit salad with scoops of mango sorbet or pineapple ice-cream. Chop the fruit into smaller chunks first.

ginger and orange pudding

2

2-4 hrs **HIGH**

Custard or cream

Chef's note

Nothing beats a proper steamed pudding and the slow cooker makes these with ease! This pudding is bound to become a firm favourite and is perfect fare on a chilly autumnal day.

V

Suitable for Vegetarians

50 g/2 oz/¼ cup **butter**, softened, plus extra for greasing

1 **orange**

50 g/2 oz/¼ cup **caster (superfine) sugar**

50 g/2 oz/½ cup **self-raising flour**

2.5 ml/½ tsp **ground ginger**

1 **egg**, lightly beaten

15 g/½ oz **stem ginger**, finely chopped

1   Grease a 600 ml/1 pint/2½ cup pudding basin with butter, then line the base with a circle of non-stick baking parchment. Place an upturned saucer or metal pastry (paste) cutter in the base of the ceramic cooking pot and pour in about 2.5 cm/1 in of very hot (not boiling) water. Switch on the slow cooker to High.

2   Grate the zest off the orange on a grater or using a zester. Cut the orange in half and squeeze out 15 ml/1 tbsp of the juice. Put the grated zest, butter and sugar in a bowl and beat together until creamy. Sift the flour and ground ginger over, then add the egg, stem ginger and orange juice. Beat everything together until well mixed.

3   Spoon and scrape the mixture into the prepared basin. Cover the pudding with a piece of pleated, lightly greased baking parchment, followed by pleated foil, tucking the excess paper and foil tightly under the rim. Place the pudding on the saucer or pastry cutter in the pot and pour in enough boiling water to come half-way up the side of the basin.

4   Cover with the lid and cook for 2–4 hours or until the pudding is well risen and firm. Turn out the pudding and remove the lining paper. Serve half of the pudding hot with custard or cream.

Second serving
- Allow the second portion of pudding to cool, then cover and keep in the fridge for the following day. Serve cold, or reheat in an ovenproof dish covered with foil in a low oven or covered with clingfilm (plastic wrap) in the microwave.

Cook's tip
- For a lemon ginger pudding, replace the orange with a large lemon. The pudding will have a sharper flavour, so spoon over a little golden (corn) or ginger syrup from the stem ginger when serving, if liked.

rich christmas pudding

2

4 hrs LOW

Custard, brandy sauce or rum butter

175 g/6 oz/1 cup **luxury dried mixed fruit** (fruit cake mix)

30 ml/2 tbsp **sherry, brandy, rum** or an **orange liqueur**

50 g/2 oz/¼ cup **butter**, softened, plus extra for greasing

50 g/2 oz/¼ cup **dark muscovado sugar**

1 **egg**, lightly beaten

25 g/1 oz **chopped nuts** such as almonds (or add extra fruit if you prefer)

25 g/1 oz/¼ cup **self-raising flour**

1.5 ml/¼ tsp **mixed (apple-pie) spice**

1.5 ml/¼ tsp **ground cinnamon**

1.5 ml/¼ tsp **ground ginger**

25 g/1 oz/½ cup **fresh white breadcrumbs**

1   Put the dried fruit and alcohol in a bowl, stir and leave to soak while preparing the rest of the ingredients.

2   Place an upturned saucer or a metal pastry (paste) cutter in the base of the ceramic cooking pot. Pour in about 5 cm/2 in of hot (not boiling) water, then turn on the slow cooker to Auto. Grease a 750 ml/1¼ pint/3 cup pudding basin.

3   Beat together the butter and sugar in a bowl until light and fluffy, then beat in the eggs, fruit and nuts. Sift the flour and spices over, then stir into the egg mixture with the breadcrumbs.

4   Spoon the mixture into the prepared basin and smooth the top. Cover with a double thickness of greaseproof (waxed) paper, pleated in the middle to allow the pudding to expand. Cover with a sheet of foil and tie with string.

5   Place the basin on top of the saucer or pastry cutter in the pot, then pour in enough boiling water to come two-thirds up the side of the basin. Cover with the lid and cook for 4 hours.

6   Remove from the pan, leave until cold, then store in a cool, dry place for at least 2 weeks and up to 3 months.

7   Reheat as before in the slow cooker for 1 hour and serve half with custard, brandy sauce or rum butter. Leave the other portion to cool, cover and keep in the fridge for up to 3 days.

Second serving
- Reheat the second portion for about 2 minutes on High in the microwave.

Cook's tip
- 'Luxury' dried mixed fruit contains a mixture of sultanas (golden raisins), currants and raisins as well as chopped dried apricots, pineapple, cherries and citrus peel.

moist banana and orange cake

Chef's note

This delicious cake is an excellent way to use up an over-ripe banana and is perfect with a cup of coffee or tea mid-morning or late afternoon. Amazingly, the mixture darkens to an attractive rich dark brown colour as it cooks. It's finished with a crunchy sugar topping, or you could add a coconut frosting as suggested below.

V

Suitable for Vegetarians

100 g/4 oz/1 cup **plain (all-purpose) flour**

2.5 ml/½ tsp **bicarbonate of soda** (baking soda)

1.5 ml/¼ tsp **cream of tartar**

50 g/2 oz/¼ cup **butter**

75 g/3 oz/⅓ cup **caster (superfine) sugar**

30 ml/2 tbsp **orange juice**

1 **banana**, mashed, around 150 g/5 oz

1 **egg**, lightly beaten

15 ml/1 tbsp **demerara** or **granulated sugar**

1. Place an upturned saucer or a metal pastry (paste) cutter in the base of the ceramic cooking pot. Pour in about 5 cm/2 in of hot (not boiling) water, then turn on the slow cooker to High. Grease a 13–15 cm/5–6 in round fixed-base cake tin or soufflé dish and line the base with greaseproof (waxed) paper or baking parchment.

2. Put the flour, bicarbonate of soda and cream of tartar in a bowl. Cut the butter into cubes and rub it in until the mixture resembles breadcrumbs. Stir in the caster sugar. Alternatively, put all the dry ingredients (including the caster sugar) in a food processor, add the cubed butter and whiz together.

3. Mix together the orange juice and banana, then stir in the egg. Stir into the dry ingredients (or add to the food processor) and mix together to combine.

4. Spoon the mixture into the prepared tin or dish and level the top. Sprinkle with the demerara or granulated sugar. Cover the dish with clingfilm (plastic wrap) or lightly greased foil and place on top of the saucer or pastry cutter in the pot. Pour in enough boiling water to come half-way up the side of the dish or tin.

5. Cover with the lid and cook for 2 hours or until the cake is well risen and firm and a skewer inserted into the middle comes out clean. Carefully remove from the slow cooker and stand on a cooling rack for 5 minutes before turning out.

Cook's tip

- For a simple coconut frosting, don't sprinkle the top of the cake with demerara sugar before cooking. Beat together 25 g/1 oz/2 tbsp of unsalted (sweet) butter with 50 g/2 oz/⅓ cup of sifted icing (confectioners') sugar and 10 ml/2 tsp of coconut liqueur. Spread over the top of the cooled cake and scatter with dried banana chips and coconut flakes.

dark and sticky gingerbread

50 g/2 oz/¼ cup **butter** or **sunflower magarine**

75 g/3 oz/⅓ cup **light brown sugar**

40 g/1½ oz **black treacle (molasses)**

40 g/1½ oz **golden (light corn) syrup**

75 g/3 oz/¾ cup **self-raising flour**

5 ml/1 tsp **ground ginger**

1 **egg**, lightly beaten

25 g/1 oz chopped **preserved ginger** (optional)

1.5 ml/¼ tsp **bicarbonate of soda** (baking soda)

100 ml/3½ oz/scant ½ cup **milk**

1   Place an upturned saucer or a metal pastry (paste) cutter in the base of the ceramic cooking pot. Pour in about 5 cm/2 in of hot (not boiling) water, then turn on the slow cooker to High. Grease a 13–15 cm/5–6 in round fixed-base cake tin or soufflé dish and line the base with greaseproof (waxed) paper or baking parchment.

2   Cut the butter or margarine into chunks and put in a heatproof bowl (check first that it will fit comfortably in the ceramic cooking pot). Add the sugar, treacle and syrup. Cover with a lid and leave for 15 minutes or until the butter has melted.

3   Remove the bowl from the slow cooker and stir the melted ingredients together. Sift the flour and ginger over and stir into the mixture with the egg and chopped ginger, if using.

4   Blend the bicarbonate of soda with a little of the milk, then stir in the rest of the milk. Add to the bowl and stir until well blended. Pour the mixture into the prepared tin or dish and cover with clingfilm (plastic wrap) or lightly greased foil. Place in the cooking pot on top of the saucer or pastry cutter.

5   Pour in enough boiling water to come about half-way up the side of the tin or dish. Cover and cook for 3–4 hours or until a skewer inserted into the middle comes out clean. Remove from the slow cooker and allow to stand on a cooling rack for 10 minutes, then turn out and leave to cool. Peel off the lining paper. Store in an airtight tin for up to 5 days.

Cook's tips
- This cake is also delicious served as a dessert with custard.
- Use this recipe to make a sticky cinnamon cake by leaving out the ginger and substituting 5 ml/1 tsp of ground cinnamon. Use extra golden syrup instead of the black treacle or molasses.

double chocolate cake

4

2 hrs HIGH

Chef's note

This moist, dark chocolate cake dotted with chocolate chips surpasses any oven-baked version and is beautifully even-textured. It is finished with a thick, shiny chocolate glaze but, if you prefer, dust the top with a mixture of cocoa powder and icing (confectioners') sugar instead.

For the cake:

65 g/2½ oz/⅓ cup **butter**, softened, plus extra for greasing

40 g/1½ oz/3 tbsp **light brown sugar**

15 g/½ oz **clear honey**

50 g/2 oz/½ cup **self-raising flour**

20 ml/1½ tbsp **cocoa (unsweetened chocolate) powder**

1.5 ml/¼ tsp **baking powder**

1 **egg**, lightly beaten

5 ml/1 tsp **vanilla essence** (extract)

50 g/2 oz/½ cup **plain (semi-sweet) chocolate chips**

For the chocolate glaze:

50 g/2 oz/½ cup **plain chocolate chips**

45 ml/3 tbsp **double (heavy) cream**

7.5 ml/½ tbsp **golden (light corn) syrup**

1   Place an upturned saucer or a metal pastry (paste) cutter in the base of the ceramic cooking pot. Pour in about 5 cm/2 in of hot (not boiling) water, then turn on the slow cooker to High. Grease a 13–15 cm/5–6 in round fixed-base cake tin and line the base with baking parchment.

2   To make the cake, put the butter, sugar and honey in a bowl and mix until just combined. Sift the flour, cocoa powder and baking powder over and add the egg and vanilla essence. Beat everything together for a minute or two until thoroughly combined. Alternatively, put all the ingredients in a food processor and whiz together for about 30 seconds. Stir in the chocolate chips.

3   Spoon and scrape the mixture into the prepared tin and level the top. Cover the dish with clingfilm (plastic wrap) or with lightly greased foil and place on top of the saucer or pastry cutter in the pot. Pour in enough boiling water to come half-way up the sides of the tin.

4   Cover with the lid and cook for 2 hours or until the cake is well risen and firm and a skewer inserted into the middle comes out clean. Turn off the slow cooker, then carefully remove the cake and stand on a cooling rack for 5 minutes before turning out.

5   Meanwhile, to make the chocolate glaze, put a heatproof bowl in the hot water in the ceramic cooking pot. Add all the glaze ingredients and leave until melted, then stir together. Leave the glaze in the slow cooker until the cake is cold (as the water cools the glaze will thicken a little). Spoon over the top of the cake, letting some drizzle down the sides as well.

cappuccino cake

3-4

2 hrs HIGH

For the cake:

10 ml/2 tsp **instant espresso coffee powder**

15 ml/1 tbsp near-boiling **water**

50 g/2 oz/¼ cup **butter**, softened

50 g/2 oz/¼ cup **caster (superfine) sugar**

1 large **egg**, lightly beaten

50 g/2 oz/½ cup **self-raising flour**

For the frosting:

10 ml/2 tsp **instant espresso coffee powder**

100 g/4 oz/½ cup **Mascarpone cheese**

5 ml/1 tsp **caster (superfine) sugar**

5 ml/1 tsp **drinking chocolate powder**

1   Place an upturned saucer or a metal pastry (paste) cutter in the base of the ceramic cooking pot. Pour in about 5 cm/2 in of hot (not boiling) water, then turn on the slow cooker to High. Grease a 13–15 cm/5–6 in round fixed-base cake tin with butter and line the base with baking parchment.

2   To make the cake, blend the espresso powder and near-boiling water in a bowl, then add the butter and sugar and beat together for a minute. Add the beaten egg and sift the flour over. Beat for a further minute or until everything is combined. Alternatively, put all the ingredients in a food processor (mix the coffee powder and water together first) and whiz together for 30 seconds.

3   Spoon and scrape the mixture into the prepared tin and level the top. Cover with clingfilm (plastic wrap) or lightly greased foil and place on top of the saucer or pastry cutter in the pot. Pour in enough boiling water to come half-way up the side of the tin.

4   Cover with the lid and cook for 2 hours or until the cake is well risen and firm and a skewer inserted into the middle comes out clean. Carefully remove from the slow cooker and stand on a cooling rack for 5 minutes before turning out.

5   To make the frosting, put the espresso powder, Mascarpone and sugar in a mixing bowl and beat together until thoroughly blended. Spread the frosting over the top of the cake and dust with the drinking chocolate powder.

Cook's tip
• The cake should be stored in the fridge, preferably in an airtight container. It will keep for up to 3 days. The cake will freeze beautifully, but the icing isn't suitable for freezing, so ice it during or after thawing.

index

apricot
   lamb and apricot tagine 122–3
   spicy pork and apricots 132–3
asparagus
   risotto verde 204–5
aubergine
   lamb with aubergines 112–13
   mediterranean vegetable stew 224–5

bacon
   barley, bacon and sausages 148–9
baked beans, chilli 198–9
banana and orange cake, moist 242–3
barley, bacon and sausages 148–9
beans
   chilli bean chowder 24–5
   chilli with chorizo 142–3
   turkey and bean cassoulet 184–5
   see also specific beans
beef
   beef in red wine 108–9
   crumble-topped beef casserole 94–5
   frikadellers 104–5
   goulash with caraway seeds 102–3
   greek stifado 98–9
   mid-week pork meatloaf 96–7
   new england braised beef 90–91
   south american beef pot 100–101
   spiced beef with horseradish 92–3
black treacle
   boston baked beans 46–7
   dark and sticky gingerbread 244–5
black-eyed beans
   caribbean-style chicken 180–81
   chilli with chorizo 142–3

blueberry panettone 234–5
boston baked beans 46–7
braised lamb with cannellini 114–15
braised turbot in white wine 80–81
bread
   cheese and cannellini bake 194–5
   cheesy bread pudding 56–7
   chicken meat balls with rice 166–7
   crunchy garlic bread topping 185
   rich christmas pudding 240–41
broad beans
   greek stifado 98–9
   risotto verde 204–5
butter beans
   butter bean and pesto soup 32–3
   butter bean bake 222–3
butternut squash
   split pea and squash soup 40–41

cabbage
   goulash with caraway seeds 102–3
   new england braised beef 90–91
cannellini beans
   boston baked beans 46–7
   braised lamb with cannellini 114–15
   cheese and cannellini bake 194–5
   spiced bean and pumpkin stew 206–7
cannelloni, tuna 76–7
capers, cod with onions and 72–3
cappucino cake 248–9
caribbean-style chicken 180–81
carrots
   braised lamb with cannellini 114–15
   cheese and lentil loaf 200–201
   goulash with caraway seeds 102–3

ham hock and lentil braise 144–5
lamb with carrots and barley 118–19
lamb with dill and vegetables 126–7
meat-free bolognese 218–19
mid-week pork meatloaf 96–7
rich lentil and tomato soup 34–5
sausage supper 146–7
simple irish stew 110–11
venison with cranberries 152–3
cashew nuts
chicken and cashew biryani 172–3
hot cashew and spinach rice 212–13
celery
barley, bacon and sausages 148–9
duck with orange sauce 190–91
jambalaya 164–5
rich lentil and tomato soup 34–5
cheese
butter bean bake 272–3
cheese and cannellini bake 194–5
cheese and lentil loaf 200–201
cheesy bread pudding 56–7
chilli tomato cheese and bread
pudding 57
grilled vegetable bake 52–3
harissa-spiced chick peas 54–5
mushroom and tuna pasta 86–7
see also cream cheese
cherry custard pots 228–9
chick peas
chicken masala soup 36–7
harissa-spiced chick peas 54–5
chicken
caribbean-style chicken 180–81
chicken and cashew biryani 172–3
chicken in red pepper sauce 162–3
chicken masala soup 36–7
chicken meat balls with rice 166–7
chilli chicken and chorizo rice 174–5
coq au vin 170–71
creamy chicken pâté 50–51

ginger chicken and pineapple 158–9
honey mustard chicken 178–9
hot and spicy mexican chicken 168–9
jambalaya 164–5
normandy chicken 160–61
one-pot chicken casserole 156–7
savoury chicken and rice 48–9
chilli baked beans 198–9
chilli bean chowder 24–5
chilli chicken and chorizo rice 174–5
chilli with chorizo 142–3
chilli tomato cheese and bread
pudding 57
chinese braised lamb 120–21
chocolate
chocolate pudding 232–3
chocolate rice pudding 230–31
chocolate sauce 232–3
double chocolate cake 246–7
chorizo
chilli chicken and chorizo rice 174–5
chilli with chorizo 142–3
classic vichyssoise 28–9
cocoa powder
chocolate pudding 232–3
chocolate rice pudding 230–31
double chocolate cake 246–7
cod with onions and capers 72–3
coffee powder
cappucino cake 248–9
comforting turkey casserole 186–7
coq au vin 170–71
corn see sweetcorn
cornbread topping 198–9
cornish hen see poussin
crab and corn chowder 64–5
cranberry
venison with cranberries 152–3
cream cheese
luxury fish pie 70–71
salmon and dill mousse 66–7

creamy chicken pâté 50–51
créme fraîche
    crab and corn chowder 64–5
    creamy chicken pâté 50–51
    macaroni cheese 44–5
    mixed fish terrine 58–9
crumble-topped beef casserole 94–5
cucumber raita 124–5

dark and sticky gingerbread 244–5
double chocolate cake 246–7
duck with orange sauce 190–91
dumplings 102–3

easy salmon risotto 78–9
easy vegetable lasagne 214–15
egg, lentil and coconut curry 196–7

fish
    luxury fish pie 70–71
    mixed fish terrine 58–9
    see also specific fish
french beans
    spiced bean and pumpkin stew 206–7
french onion soup 38–9
fresh swordfish with lentils 74–5
frikadellers 104
fruit
    rich christmas pudding 240–41
    tropical fruit salad 236–7
    tropical fruit sundae 237

ginger
    dark and sticky gingerbread 244–5
    ginger and orange pudding 238–9
    ginger chicken and pineapple 158–9
    lemon ginger pudding 239
golden syrup
    dark and sticky gingerbread 244–5
    double chocolate cake 246–7
goulash with caraway seeds 102–3

greek stifado 98–9
grilled vegetable bake 52–3

haddock
    luxury fish pie 70–71
    smoked haddock kedgeree 62–3
ham hock and lentil braise 144–5
haricot beans
spiced bean and pumpkin stew 206–7
harissa paste
    harissa-spiced chick peas 54–5
    lamb and apricot tagine 122–3
hoisin sauce
    chinese braised lamb 120–21
honey mustard chicken 178–9
hot and spicy mexican chicken 168–9
hungarian sausage soup 26–7

jambalaya 164–5

kidney beans
    chilli baked beans 198–9
    chilli bean chowder 24–5
king prawn and spinach balti 84–5

lamb
    braised lamb with cannellini 114–15
    chinese braised lamb 120–21
    lamb and apricot tagine 122–3
    lamb and lentil curry 124–5
    lamb and sweet potato stew 116–17
    lamb with aubergines 112–13
    lamb with carrots and barley 118–19
    lamb with dill and vegetables 126–7
    lancashire hotpot 128–9
    simple irish stew 110–11
lancashire hotpot 128–9
leeks
    classic vichyssoise 28
    lancashire hotpot 128–9
lemon ginger pudding 239

lentils
  cheese and lentil loaf 200–201
  egg, lentil and coconut curry 196–7
  fresh swordfish with lentils 74–5
  ham hock and lentil braise 144–5
  lamb and lentil curry 124–5
  red lentil and vegetable dhal 210–11
  rich lentil and tomato soup 34–5
luxury fish pie 70–71

macaroni cheese 44–5
maple syrup
spicy maple ribs 140–41
mauritian vegetable curry 208–9
meat-free bolognese 218–19
mediterranean vegetable stew 224–5
mexican pork tacos 138–9
mexican spice tomato purée 169
mid-week pork meatloaf 96–7
milk
  blueberry panettone 234–5
  cheesy bread pudding 56–7
  cherry custard pots 228–9
  chocolate rice pudding 230–31
  grilled vegetable bake 52–3
mince, savoury 106–7
mini sausages
  barley, bacon and sausages 148–9
  sausage supper 146–7
mixed beans
  mixed bean hotpot 220–21
  turkey and bean cassoulet 184–5
  see also beans
mixed fish terrine 58–9
mixed vegetable soup 22–3
moist banana and orange cake 242–3
mushrooms
  beef in red wine 108–9
  chinese braised lamb 120–21
  comforting turkey casserole 186–7

coq au vin 170–71
meat-free bolognese 218–19
mediterranean vegetable stew 224–5
mixed bean hotpot 220–21
mushroom and tuna paste 86–7
turkey cacciatore 188–9
wild mushroom risotto 202–3
wild mushroom soup 30–31

nam pla fish sauce
  thai-spiced pork with veg 136–7
new england braised beef 90–91
normandy chicken 160–61

one-pot chicken casserole 156–7
onion
  boston baked beans 46–7
  chicken and cashew biryani 172–3
  cod with onions and capers 72–3
  fresh onion soup 38–9
  lamb with dill and vegetables 126–7
  lancashire hotpot 128–9
orange
  duck with orange sauce 190–91
  ginger and orange pudding 238–9
  moist banana and orange cake 242–3

panettone, blueberry 234–5
pasta, mushroom and tuna 86–7
pear
  poussin with pear stuffing 176–7
pearl barley
  barley, bacon and sausages 148–9
  lamb and sweet potato stew 116–17
peas
  barley, bacon and sausages 148–9
  chicken and cashew biryani 172–3
  chicken meat balls with rice 166–7
  comforting turkey casserole 186–7
  luxury fish pie 70–71

thai turkey curry 182–3
tuna cannelloni 76–7
pepperami sausage
  chilli chicken and chorizo rice 174–5
  jambalaya 164–5
peppers
  chicken in red pepper sauce 162–3
  frikadellers 104–5
  hot and spicy mexican chicken 168–9
  hungarian sausage soup 26–7
  jambalaya 164–5
  mediterranean vegetable stew 224–5
  mexican pork tacos 138–9
  one-pot chicken casserole 156–7
  savoury chicken and rice 48–9
  south american beef pot 100–101
  thai-spiced pork with veg 136–7
pesto sauce
  butter bean and pesto soup 32–3
pineapple
  ginger chicken and pineapple 158–9
  sweet and sour quorn 216–17
  tropical fruit salad 236–7
pinto beans
  chilli with chorizo 142–3
pork
  frikadellers 104–5
  mexican pork tacos 138–9
  mid-week pork meatloaf 96–7
  pork with apple and red
    cabbage 130–31
  pork chops in barbecue sauce 134–5
  spicy maple ribs 140–41
  spicy pork and apricots 132–3
  thai-spiced pork with veg 136–7
pork sausage
  boston baked beans 46–7
  hungarian sausage soup 26–7
potato
  classic vichyssoise 28
  crab and corn chowder 64–5
  duck with orange sauce 190–91

greek stifado 98–9
lamb with dill and vegetables 126–7
lancashire hotpot 128–9
luxury fish pie 70–71
mixed bean hotpot 220–21
new england braised beef 90–91
one-pot chicken casserole 156–7
sausage and potato pot 150–51
sausage supper 146–7
simple irish stew 110–11
south american beef pot 100–101
thai turkey curry 182–3
poussin
  poussin with pear stuffing 176–7
prawns
  jambalaya 164–5
  king prawn and spinach balti 84–5
  luxury fish pie 70–71
pumpkin
  spiced bean and pumpkin stew 206–7

quorn, sweet and sour 216–17

ratatouille
  easy vegetable lasagne 214–15
red cabbage
  pork with apple and red
    cabbage 130–31
red lentil and vegetable dhal 210–11
red wine
  beef in red wine 108–9
  coq au vin 170–71
  greek stifado 98–9
rice
  chicken and cashew biryani 172–3
  chicken meat balls with rice 166–7
  chilli chicken and chorizo rice 174–5
  chocolate rice pudding 230–31
  easy salmon risotto 78–9
  hot cashew and spinach rice 212–13
  rice puddings 230–31
  risotto verde 204–5

savoury chicken and rice 48–9
simple seafood paella 62–3
smoked haddock kedgeree 62–3
wild mushroom risotto 202–3
rich christmas pudding 240–41
rich lentil and tomato soup 34–5
risotto verde 204–5

salmon
easy salmon risotto 78–9
mixed fish terrine 58–9
salmon and dill mousse 66–7
spicy salmon steak 68–9
sausage see chorizo; French sausage;
mini
sausages; pepperami sausage;
pork sausage
savoury chicken and rice 48–9
savoury mince 106–7
seafood
simple seafood paella 62–3
simple irish stew 110–11
simple seafood paella 62–3
smoked haddock kedgeree 62–3
south american beef pot 100–101
soya mince
meat-free bolognese 218–19
spiced bean and pumpkin stew 206–7
spiced beef with horseradish 92–3
spicy maple ribs 140–41
spicy pork and apricots 132–3
spinach
harissa-spiced chick peas 54–5
hot cashew and spinach rice 212–13
king prawn and spinach balti 84–5
split pea and squash soup 40–41
sticky cinnamon cake 245
stroganoff sauce 167
sweet potato
lamb and sweet potato stew 116–17
spiced bean and pumpkin stew 206–7
split pea and squash soup 40–41

sweet and sour quorn 216–17
sweetcorn
crab and corn chowder 64–5
luxury fish pie 70–71
mexican pork tacos 138–9
swordfish with lentils, fresh 74–5

thai turkey curry 182–3
thai-spiced pork with veg 136–7
tomato
braised lamb with cannellini 114–15
chicken in red pepper sauce 162–3
chicken masala soup 36–7
chicken meat balls with rice 166–7
chilli tomato cheese and bread
pudding 57
chilli with chorizo 142–3
crumble-topped beef casserole 94–5
easy salmon risotto 78–9
frikadellers 104–5
goulash with caraway seeds 102–3
greek stifado 98–9
harissa-spiced chick peas 54–5
hungarian sausage soup 26–7
lamb with aubergines 112–13
meat-free bolognese 218–19
mediterranean vegetable stew 224–5
mexican pork tacos 138–9
one-pot chicken casserole 156–7
rich lentil and tomato soup 34–5
sausage and potato pot 150–51
savoury chicken and rice 48–9
savoury mince 106–7
tuna cannelloni 76–7
turkey and bean cassoulet 184–5
turkey cacciatore 188–9
tropical fruit salad 236–7
trout
mixed fish terrine 58–9
tuna
mushroom and tuna paste 86–7
tuna cannelloni 76–7

turbot in white wine, braised 80–81
turkey
    comforting turkey casserole 186–7
    sausage and potato pot 150–51
    thai turkey curry 182–3
    turkey and bean cassoulet 184–5
    turkey cacciatore 188–9

vegetables
    butter bean and pesto soup 32–3
    chicken and cashew biryani 172–3
    chilli chicken and chorizo rice 174–5
    comforting turkey casserole 186–7
    crumble-topped beef casserole 94–5
    easy vegetable lasagne 214–15
    greek stifado 98–9
    grilled vegetable bake 52–3
    hungarian sausage soup 26–7
    lamb with dill and vegetables 126–7
    lancashire hotpot 128–9

mauritian vegetable curry 208–9
mediterranean vegetable stew 224–5
new england braised beef 90–91
one-pot chicken casserole 156–7
red lentil and vegetable dhal 210–11
simple irish stew 110–11
sweet and sour quorn 216–17
thai-spiced pork with veg 136–7
see also mixed vegetables; specific
    vegetables
venison with cranberries 152–3

white sauce 215
white wine
    braised turbot in white wine 80–81
    easy salmon risotto 78–9
    french onion soup 38
    risotto verde 204–5
wild mushroom risotto 202–3
wild mushroom soup 30–31